THE
POWER
OF
TRANSCENDENCE

GROWING IN LOVE, CREATIVITY, HEALTH, AND HAPPINESS

ANN PURCELL

GREEN DRAGON BOOKS

Green Dragon Books
Palm Beach, Florida, USA

Transcendental Meditation®, TM®, TM-Sidhi®, Yogic Flying®, Maharishi School of the Age of Enlightenment®, Maharishi University of Management®, Maharishi Ayurveda, Transcendental Meditation Sidhi Program, Consciousness-Based Education, Consciousness-Based, Maharishi Vedic Science, and Mother Divine Program are protected trademarks and are used in the U.S. under license or with permission.

Green Dragon Books
PO Box 1608
Lake Worth, FL 33460 USA
www.greendragonbooks.com
info@greendragonbooks.com

ISBN 1623860520
paperback 9781623860523
ebook 9781623860530

Library of Congress Cataloging in Publication # 2017002149

DEDICATION

This book is dedicated to

YOU

and everyone who desires a better world

and is seeking a deeper, more meaningful quality of life.

CONTENTS

INTRODUCTION

On November 11, 1972, a simple event forever altered the trajectory of my life. On that day I had my first experience of transcendence. I had never felt so deep, silent, and peaceful, yet at the same time totally awake inside. On the way home after my first session of learning Transcendental Meditation® (TM®) I felt a huge weight had been lifted off me. All of nature around me felt vibrant and seemed to be smiling at me. I knew something profound had happened.

In 1973 I became a teacher of Transcendental Meditation and, on the basis of the many immediate positive changes I noticed, have devoted my entire adult life to sharing the benefits of TM in America and around the world.

Why am I so passionate about this natural, effortless practice? It's simple—because it works. When I first learned TM it was considered a fad, and there was very little scientific research that documented its effects. Since that time, TM has been taught to over half a million students in schools around the world and to people from all walks of life. Veterans with post-traumatic stress disorder (PTSD), inner-city children, prisoners, business people, mothers and fathers, doctors, and other health professionals are all enjoying the many benefits of TM.

Scores of celebrities have been practicing for decades. Jerry Seinfeld and Howard Stern both learned TM when they were eighteen years old. Paul McCartney, Ringo Starr, Donovan, and Mike Love all learned in the late 1960s. Clint Eastwood learned in the early 1970s. All of these talented, accomplished people are still avid practitioners.

Other celebrities who have learned TM and publicly shared the benefits of their practice include: Katy Perry, Sting, Oprah Winfrey, David Lynch, Dr. Mehmet Oz, Cameron Diaz, Hugh Jackman, Ivanka Trump, Gwyneth Paltrow, Jennifer Aniston, Russell Brand, Sheryl Crow, Ellen DeGeneres, Ray Dalio, Laura Dern, Lena Dunham, Ben Foster, Judy Greer, Heather Graham, Sean Lennon, Eva Mendes, James McCartney, Rick Rubin, Robin Roberts, George Stephanopoulos, Amy Schumer, Martin Scorsese, Liv Tyler, and Naomi Watts. The list goes on.

Mainstream acceptance of TM is also now prevalent in the field of healthcare, educational institutions, the military, and prisons. TM has been incorporated into recovery programs for abused women, people with AIDS, the homeless, and first responders with post-traumatic stress.

How can a technique that is so simple be so tremendously effective? I believe it is because Transcendental Meditation is completely natural. TM uses the natural tendency of the mind to automatically go to what is more pleasing. If your favorite music comes on in the next room, your mind will automatically go there without any effort at all. The Transcendental Meditation technique uses this natural tendency by turning the mind inward to go to a field of greater happiness.

Given the right vehicle or opportunity, the mind will automatically go to quieter, more charming levels of thinking until it reaches the most quiet level, the transcendent, the deepest level of our being. Research shows that the experience of transcendence creates coherence between the left and right hemispheres of the brain. Increased brain wave coherence is associated with more integrated and effective thinking and behavior, including greater intelligence, creativity, learning ability, emotional stability, ethical and moral reasoning, self-confidence, and reduced anxiety.

When the mind settles down to this most coherent state of brain functioning, the body also settles and receives a profound state of rest, which allows stress to be released. Stress has been called the plague of the 21st century. As scientific studies have repeatedly confirmed, reducing stress in our mind and physiology has profound health benefits.

More than 360 peer-reviewed published studies conducted in over 250 independent research universities in thirty different countries document the vast array of improvements in mind, body, and behavior through practice of Transcendental Meditation.

The transcendental level of awareness is a state of calm, order, and most of all, pure joy—I'll even say bliss. The ancient Vedic Literature calls this transcendental state *samādhi* and *ānanda*—Sanskrit words referring to a peaceful state of mind and bliss. Christ said, "The Kingdom of Heaven is within." Buddha talked about *nirvana*. In the Koran, there is the concept of *jannah*—the garden of bliss. In the *Tao Te Ching*, Laozi talks about the "One" and states "by realizing the One, Heaven becomes clear . . ."

I wrote a book to share the universal journey of growing in inner fulfillment. *The Transcendental Meditation Technique and the Journey of Enlightenment* was the result of this endeavor.

After the book was released, I was advised by my social media expert and publisher to write at least two blogs weekly to inspire people to visit my website and learn more about the book. Through a fortuitous set of events, Arianna Huffington invited me to blog for her popular news website, The Huffington Post. Thus, my life as a blogger began.

I quickly discovered that I love blogging. It is a means for me to explore meditation, enlightenment, and spirituality from many different angles, and to reflect on deeply personal experiences, the creative process, health, and well-being. The blogs I write also consider the deeper meaning of love, yoga, happiness, the concept of heaven and God, and holistic solutions to the many problems facing the world today. This new book is a compilation of many of the blogs that I have published online over the last five years. The posts have been slightly edited for repetition and are presented in a more condensed format. Please see the notes section at the back of the book for a complete list of where each blog was originally published online, as well as internal reference notes.

My desire is that reading this book will expand your awareness, deepen your insights into life, uplift your heart, and, most importantly, give you a concrete vision and path towards creating a better world.

Transcending and experiencing the field of pure silence through the TM technique may be the most scientifically validated and powerful way to transform individual lives and nations. With the present chaotic state of global affairs, now is the time to explore this possibility to create a more peaceful and heavenly world.

May you experience transcendence in your life and grow in love, creativity, health, and happiness.

Ann Purcell

THE POWER OF
TRANSCENDENCE

I have seen the transformative power of transcendence in my own life, but how can its power be explained to someone else? Transcending is an abstract experience whereby one fathoms finer and finer levels of the thinking process until one transcends the finest level of thinking and experiences the source of all thought—the purest level of consciousness. Transcendence is an unbounded state of awareness, where consciousness expands to embrace infinity. It is like a wave settling down into the vast, calm ocean.

Does the experience of transcendence have the power to change our society?

Anwar Sadat's Spiritual Transformation

The former President of Egypt, Anwar Sadat, described a beautiful transformative experience of transcendence. As a military officer during World War II, before becoming president, he plotted to free Egypt from British rule. He was imprisoned because of these activities. In his autobiography, *In Search of Identity*, he recounts his experiences of solitary confinement, during which he was completely cut off from any links to the outside world, including radio and newspapers. The only companionship he had during that time was his inner entity, which he called "self."

I was able to transcend the confines of time and place. Spatially, I did not live in a four-walled cell but in the entire universe. Time ceased to exist once my heart was taken over by the love of the Lord of all Creation: I came to feel very close to Him wherever I was . . .[1]

The Transformation

Experiencing transcendence caused Anwar Sadat to change the course of his leadership objectives from hate to love:

For now I felt I had stepped into a vaster and more beautiful world and my capacity for endurance redoubled. I felt I could stand the pressure, whatever the magnitude of a given problem. My paramount object was to make people happy. To see someone smile, to feel that another man's heart beat for joy, was to me a source of immeasurable happiness. I identified with people's joys. Such despicable emotions as hate and vengeance were banished as the faith that "right" ultimately triumphs came to be ineradicably implanted in my consciousness. I came to feel more deeply than ever the beauty of love . . .

Love helped me to know myself. When my individual entity merged into the vaster entity of all existence, my point of departure became love of home (Egypt), love of all being, love of God. And so I have proceeded from love in discharging my duty (my responsibility), whether it was during my last months in prison . . . or now that I am President of Egypt.[2]

Sadat was awarded the Nobel Peace Prize for his historic efforts to create peace in the Middle East despite strong opposition from the Arab world. There are many other instances of great writers, poets, artists, and athletes who had spontaneous experiences of transcendence that changed the course of their lives to a more positive direction. However, they often were not able to repeat the experience.

The Difference between Transcendence and Silencing the Mind

It is important to understand that transcendence is very different from trying to silence the mind, or emptying your mind of thoughts. Attempting to silence the mind in the hopes of experiencing pure consciousness is extremely difficult. I have had so many people tell me that they tried to empty their mind of thoughts, but just felt restless and frustrated because they could not do it. They concluded that they were not able to meditate.

Everyone has the transcendent within themselves and through techniques like TM, it can be easily and effortlessly experienced. During instruction in Transcendental Meditation, one is taught how to effortlessly dive into the state of Being. One just needs to learn the technique and the dive happens automatically.

Our world desperately needs leaders who can work together to solve the problems facing each nation. However, we don't want our leaders to have to be sentenced to solitary confinement in order to transcend! In normal surroundings with the daily experience of effortless transcending, they will be better equipped to take their country in a more positive direction.

Calling All Leaders to Transcend

Imagine if all the congressmen and senators started their day by meditating together for twenty minutes. At least while meditating they would be coherent—all together enjoying the transcendent—and at the same time they would be dissolving the stress that keeps them from working together productively to solve our nation's problems.

The reality of our leaders meditating together is not out of reach. United States Congressman Tim Ryan from Ohio has organized weekly meditation sessions for Congress since 2012. He says: "There is a value in having some quiet time before votes—it can help anyone make better decisions."[3] A Thursday session for staff and a Monday one for members of Congress are known as the "Quiet Time Caucus."[4]

Recently, some leaders in the British Parliament meditated together[5] at the beginning of a session to explore the potential use of meditation for education, healthcare, and rehabilitation. The group felt that before making a decision on the matter, they should first directly experience for themselves the benefits of meditation.

Maybe having our leaders come together daily in the silence of meditation is a solution to fix our dysfunctional government. I believe all other solutions for the nation will emerge from the more coherent state of mind these leaders would spontaneously develop if they did transcend. There is the power of politics, the power of money, and the power of the people, but the greatest transformative force is the power of transcendence!

SECTION 1

LOVE

Fathoming the Infinite Depths of Love

L ove is one of the great mysteries of life. It is something everyone
wants and aspires to. The first experience of love begins at birth.
We then grow to love our family, partners, grandchildren, music, art, and
the beauty of nature. Poets try to capture love in words. Musicians write
heartfelt songs expressing the joys of love as well as its sorrows.

In his book *Love and God*,[1] Maharishi Mahesh Yogi says that:

Life expresses itself through love . . .
Every wave of life is full with the ocean of love . . .
Such a life is worth living . . .
A loving heart, a heart full of love, is the precious essence of human
life . . . Love is the most precious gift of God to us.[2]

But why is it that so many of us love today and fight tomorrow? Why
do more than one in two marriages end up in divorce? Why can't we sus-
tain the tender impulses of love?

Maharishi explains that:

Those, who are restricted in their ability to love, those, whose love
flows only in restricted channels of isolated objects or individuals,
those who can only like this or that, those, who have no awareness of
universal consciousness in their hearts, are like small ponds where
the love can flow only as ripples and not as waves of the sea . . .

When a heart, shallow as a pond seeks to rise high in waves of
love, it creates a muddle and brings out the mud that was so gracefully hidden underneath.[3]

What is the so-called "mud" in this metaphor? Maharishi is referring
to the physical imbalances and abnormalities that are incurred from an
overload of stress or overwhelming pressure from the environment.
These structural and/or functional abnormalities are retained in the
mind and body.

Can we get rid of the stresses and thereby improve the depths and magnitude of our hearts? Maharishi explains that this is possible:

> By probing deep into the purity of our being. By exploring the finer regions of the impulse of love that murmurs in the silent chamber of our heart. By diving deep into the stillness of the unbounded, unfathomable ocean of love present within our hearts. By a simple technique of self-exploration or by what is commonly known as the Transcendental Meditation technique. . . .
>
> It is easy for every one of us to fathom the unfathomable magnitude of the ocean of love present within, and forever enjoy the fullness of life in the fullness of heart.[4]

These profound words from Maharishi,[5] contrasted against all the negativity we see in the world today, almost seem too good to be true. Perhaps we have been looking too much in the outward direction to find and culture the experience of love. Love rising from within is a state of being that is not dependent on anything or anyone on the outside for fulfillment. It simply is the reality of our Being. We just need to come in contact with this level of being for the inner ocean of love to begin to flow.

We know that when we are tired or pressured it is easy to say things we don't mean and do things we regret later—we can lash out at our loved ones. This is "bringing out the mud gracefully hidden underneath."

How does going inward get rid of the "mud"? During meditation, the mind settles down and fathoms quieter, more subtle levels of the thinking process. And because mind and body are intimately connected, when the body gains a state of profound rest—much deeper than ordinary relaxation during sleep—it starts to neutralize the accumulated stresses and strains and imbalances. This deep, healing rest of the physical body allows accumulated knots of emotional and physical stress to be released. With regular daily meditation practice, the whole system gradually regains more and more of its normal functioning. As the blockages of stress dissolve, and biochemical imbalances are normalized, we return to our truer self, our less-stressed self, our more relaxed and natural self, which includes the natural flow of impulses of love.

In time, the body starts to maintain a more rested, calm, and energetic style of functioning even outside of meditation, throughout the entire day. As internal stress dissolves, we become more resilient and more immune to environmental pressures that may be coming to us from family, friends, or our environment. Through meditation, we can experience more inner happiness, fulfillment, and even love flowing from within.

In *Love and God*, Maharishi explains: "Love is purity, love is innocence, love is fullness, oneness and bliss. It brings fulfillment. Love unifies the scattered ends of life and brings them all together into an integrated whole."[6]

The ancient Greek poet Virgil expressed the power of love in his *Eclogues*, composed in 37 BC: *Omnia vincit amor et nos cedamus amori*: Love conquers all things; let us all yield to love! (X. 69)

Love and Enlightenment

Everyone wants love: to be loved, and to be able to give love. From the moment of birth, babies need love to thrive. Research by Megan Gunnar, from the University of Minnesota, shows that babies who are loved in their first six months of life—held often and securely attached to their parents—do not show elevated levels of cortisol, the stress hormone, in subsequent stressful situations.[7]

Bathing and nurturing children with love from a young age helps to create integrated, happy young adults who are then able to form their own healthy relationships.

Where Does Love Begin?

A child's birth is the beginning of her journey in this world. We see children evolve through many stages of development—the terrible twos, puberty, adolescence, adulthood, and eventually, old age. There are several aspects to this development: the outer physical value, the inner mental realm, and deeper spiritual values.

Children are naturally loving and loveable. They are born with open hearts, so they are able to receive their parents' love fully and grow in that love.

We have probably all met well-adjusted, balanced, loving teenagers and adults throughout our lives. We have also met people who have many problems and struggle in their lives. Many of these problems stem from some lack of nourishment in childhood or impressions left from a traumatic, stressful event. Stress, which everyone experiences to some degree, can be a block to the full development of our creative potential, the flow of love, and our spiritual growth—enlightenment. If children can start practicing meditation at around ten, they will have an effective way to neutralize future stress that may restrict their full development.

Stress Blocks the Flow of Love

Once we graduate from college or get a job, it can often seem that life closes in on us, especially if we get married and have children. We become more stressed, struggling to cope with life's demands. Sleep is not enough to neutralize the stresses that accumulate in mind and body over the years. Stresses block the normal functioning of heart and mind. As a result, we may feel that we are no longer growing as an individual and that our capacity for love is decreasing. How can we change this common predicament?

Education for Enlightenment

Enlightenment[8]—the development of one's full potential—should be a main goal of education, so that by the time young adults graduate, they are balanced and well-adjusted, using their full mental and creative potential to meet the challenges of life head on with joy and innovative, intelligent solutions.

An enlightened person is fully at home with herself and with who she is as a person. She can thus enjoy life both inner and outer to the fullest and is able to love and be loved with an open, receptive heart. In the state of enlightenment, a person is able to be more loving because she is not bogged down by stresses that may restrict the flow of love from her heart.

Within the silent depths of our being is an ocean of love. It is always there, we just need to tap into it. Even if we start to meditate later in life, as an adult, stresses that we have accumulated over the years will begin to dissolve and our heart will open up and be more able to flow in love. Maharishi Mahesh Yogi, founder of the Transcendental Meditation technique, explains in *Love and God* that:

> The fortunate one uses the instrument of deep meditation and probes deep into his heart. Then the waves of love gain the depth of the ocean, and the ocean of love flows and fills the heart and thrills every particle of being. Every wave of life then flows in the fullness of love, in the fullness of divine glory, in the fullness of grace, in bliss and peace.[9]

Personal Love Is Concentrated Universal Love

Maharishi goes on to explain that: "This is how, gradually, the personal love naturally moves on, to gain the status of universal love. And, this is how universal love moves on to find its expression in the personal love."[10]

Growth of enlightenment is the development of the purest state of love that exists, an inner state of Being that is not dependent on anything from the outside for its fulfillment. Love is also the most unifying, nourishing force of life.

Lord Buddha said: "If you truly loved yourself, you would never harm another."

We love our self by experiencing the deepest value of our Self, the state of purest love that exists deep within us as silence and peace. Once we have gained and stabilized this state of inner love, we are able to fulfill the following dictum beautifully stated in the Bible:

> Love is patient and kind; love does not envy or boast; it is not arrogant or rude. It does not insist on its own way; it is not irritable or resentful; it does not rejoice at wrongdoing, but rejoices with the truth. Love bears all things, believes all things, hopes all things, endures all things. Love never ends. (I Corinthians 13:4–8)

Buddha also said: "Hatred does not cease by hatred, but only by love; this is the eternal rule." As the Beatles so rightfully sang, "All you need is love."

A Moment of Pure Love

Recently, I walked down to the beach when the sun was about to rise. The ocean was a glassy silvery stillness. As I surveyed my surroundings, I knew I was not going to see the sunrise this quiet morning as there was a soft, pale, pinky-grey mountain of clouds on the distant horizon.

There were about seven or eight groups of people and a few single people sitting on beach chairs, all with hopes of seeing the first light of morning. These early-risers on the beach who had come to witness the magic of the dawn touched my heart. It was a moment of fulfillment for me, even of ecstatic joy. I felt an all-embracing love for everyone and everything around.

I don't know what unleashed this flow of bliss and love in my heart. Was it the spirit of camaraderie, the shared interest of the other people up so early to enjoy the beauty of the sun's first light? Was it the peace of the vast, silent ocean?

Whatever ignited the passion I felt for the beauty all around me, it doesn't matter. I know it was a transcendent moment where I felt the living presence of God. I am just grateful to have been at the beach that blessed morning.

SECTION 2

CREATIVITY

Transcendence and the Creative Process

When I listen to interviews with writers or musicians, the interviewer inevitably asks the question: "From where do your inspiration and creativity come?" The answers vary, but usually people will say it is a mystery, or that their inspiration came out of nowhere, or that they just write down an experience they had in daily life. Paul McCartney has said that his song "Yesterday"—one of the most famous songs written in the past century—came to him in a dream.[1]

All Creativity Comes from Within

All creativity comes from within, even if it is inspired by an outside experience. The outer experience triggers a feeling inside that unleashes the creative flow. Roger Ebert, an American film critic and historian, journalist, screenwriter and author, expresses what many artists experience in their creative process:

> When I write, I fall into the zone many writers, painters, musicians, athletes, and craftsmen of all sorts seem to share: In doing something I enjoy and am expert at, deliberate thought falls aside and it is all just *there*. I think of the next word no more than the composer thinks of the next note.[2]

What is this zone that Ebert refers to falling into? The great German composer Richard Strauss alludes to this zone in a description of his creative process:

> Composing is a procedure that is not so readily explained. When the inspiration comes, it is something of so subtle, tenuous, will-o-the-wisp-like nature that it almost defies definition. When in my most inspired moods, I have definite compelling visions, involving a higher selfhood. I feel at such moments that I am tapping the source of Infinite and Eternal energy from which you and I and all things proceed.[3]

Can anyone tap into this field of pure energy or is it only reserved for the rare creative genius?

I believe that everyone has this zone within themselves—what Strauss calls the source of infinite and eternal energy. Surprisingly, this source of infinite energy is found in the silence at the depths of our own consciousness.

What Are the Levels of Consciousness?

The surface level of the conscious mind contains our everyday thoughts, to-do lists, worries, and creative ideas. However, there are quieter levels of the conscious mind that consist of subtle feelings and intuitions.

These quieter subtle levels of consciousness are teeming with more energy, intelligence, and creativity. The subtlest level, transcendental consciousness, is beyond the field of thought and is the most silent level of our Being—an unbounded state of inner wakefulness—pure consciousness. This field of pure consciousness is equivalent to the field of infinite energy that Strauss refers to in the above quote.

How Can One Experience Being?

Fortunately, everyone can easily experience this transcendental level within through meditation. The first major change I noticed after I learned Transcendental Meditation was that I started to focus on my schoolwork, rather than on how to avoid doing my homework. The most thrilling change was the creative energy that would swell up inside me. I had to find outlets for this flow of creativity through cooking, sewing, and journaling.

I never considered myself to be a musician, writer, or poet. As a teenager, I was not an artist nor did I have any inkling towards writing. Feeling all this creative energy was a completely new experience for me. The outcome of all this energy was an outpouring of poems, songs, and now blog posts.

I can't even begin to proclaim that I write timeless, ethereal music like Strauss. However, I can describe the exhilarating joy I feel when I am experiencing this effortless flow of creativity. Sometimes it feels so effortless that I feel I am not even the writer or the composer—the song is composing itself. In fact, whenever I try to write a song or poem, it never works and feels false.

Catching the Big Fish

I notice more and more that I am catching ideas from a deeper level. In his insightful book, *Catching the Big Fish*, filmmaker David Lynch describes this process of catching ideas—the "fish"—that emerge from deep within us:

> Here's how it works: Inside every human being is an ocean of pure, vibrant consciousness. When you 'transcend' in Transcendental Meditation you dive down into that ocean of pure consciousness. You splash into it. And it's bliss. You can vibrate with this bliss. Experiencing pure consciousness enlivens it, expands it. It starts to unfold and grow . . . You can catch ideas at a deeper level. And creativity really flows. It makes life more like a fantastic game.[4]

The following are two poems that express and describe my creative process.

Poetic Flight

The page is staring at me—
blank, lifeless, and white—
waiting for my thoughts to fly free
and my pen to take poetic flight.

I see before me all possibilities—
the bubbling of pure delight—
Silence is unlocking its mysteries
like stars clustering in the night.

The direction is not yet clear
but do I need to know the way?
At this stage, I should not fear
for silence over me has sway;

always guiding me from its empty sphere—
its eternal inward play.
My tender feelings I need to hear
as they begin to unfold like a golden ray.

Silence sings its own song
from its ancient flowing hum.
Here the poet's mind belongs
from where the stirring of sound comes.

His words will then burst like the dawn
filling the page with gentle rhythms
and meanings that leap like a fawn
forming the depths of silence's wisdom.

In Silence I Hear

Tell me your wise words,
Dictate them sweetly to me.
Let them come like a rushing herd,
Or waves rolling on the sea.

My mind is still and clear,
Like the depths of a crystal pond.
In this silence I gently hear
Your words softly coming on.

In metaphors, in rhythmic rhyme
They flow like a stream.
Rising in my awareness they climb
Forming the poetry of the Supreme.

The Blank Canvas

A painter begins his painting with a blank canvas and a writer with a blank page, right? Wrong. A painter or writer begins his art from within. Even when a painter paints a beautiful scene, or a writer wants to write a story about an outside event, those ideas first resonate with some feelings within. The ideas percolate at a deeper level of the mind until they are ready to flow out onto the blank canvas. The artist brings out the inward imagination, ideas, feelings, music, and songs into the world of creation. Thus, the inner world of consciousness is the source of all creativity.

The Blank Canvas of Our Mind

From where in the mind do these creative impulses begin to emerge? There are many levels of our mind. The surface level of our mind is filled with our day-to-day thoughts—our to-do lists, dealing with present situations, and social interactions. A deeper level contains our quiet observations of what is going on around us. Intuition, feelings, and subtle, creative impulses and imagination are an even more profound level of our consciousness. The field of pure silence, Being, is beyond all these thoughts, feelings, and imagination. Just like a canvas is the blank space for an artist, silence is the pure blank canvas of everyone.

The blank canvas is a field of all possibilities. Anything can be created from the blank canvas of consciousness into any expression—artistic, athletic, commercial, etc. There are no limitations to what can be expressed. The more your awareness is open to the unbounded, limitless, blank canvas of your mind, the more you are able to draw upon this field of infinite creativity.

Contact the Field of Infinite Creativity

I did not consider myself a writer or a poet when I first learned to meditate, yet after about a year of practicing Transcendental Meditation, I started hearing melodies in my head. Sometimes words and phrases bubbled up inside. Unexpectedly, I started writing many songs and poems. The songs seemed to write themselves, as though I were just a vessel for them to flow through and emerge. My silent awareness started to burst with creativity, with words and rhythms that were embedded in my soul.

Accessing the deep silence of the mind is a fundamental means for anyone to easily release his or her inner dormant creativity. The next time you start to compose a song, paint a painting, write prose or poetry, first pull the arrow back to the blank canvas within and then let your artistic expression burst forth.

Music for Change

Poetry or songs that inspire world peace and unity have a way of bringing people together. Music is a language that transcends all boundaries and cultures, uniting everyone for a higher purpose.

Mark Johnson, who founded the organization Playing for Change,[5] said in a 2011 CNN interview:

> Music is one of the greatest ways to bring us together because it is from one heart to another heart. Regardless of all the differences of culture, race, religion, and politics, music gives us a foundation that we can build from to create something positive for the future of the planet.[6]

The people in Johnson's organization travel all around the world with a portable studio recording musicians from different countries singing and playing their local traditional instruments. They all play along with the same song while listening on headphones to the person who was recorded in the previous country. Playing for Change then takes all the different tracks back to the studio and mixes them into one cohesive song. Millions of people have enjoyed listening to these worldwide collaborations on YouTube.

Playing for Change featured on YouTube a cover of the Ben E. King classic "Stand By Me" which received over 42 million hits.[7]

Another worldwide musical collaboration was conducted by composer Eric Whitacre.[8] He led a virtual choir of 2,000 singers from around the world. The video "Sleep" went viral on YouTube[9] and is another example of people uniting through music.

Bob Marley, a great poet and composer, was literally an ambassador for world peace through his music. His much acclaimed song "One Love"[10] has been sung and performed all around the world and was picked up and recorded by Playing For Change.

The charity single "We are the World,"[11] composed in 1985 by Michael Jackson and Lionel Richie, and produced by Quincy Jones and Michael Omartian, was sung by a group of some of the most famous musicians in the world to raise funds for famine relief in Africa. The recording of this all-star performance sold over twenty million copies.

Musicians united together again for a remake of "We Are the World" in 2010 to raise millions of dollars for Haitian earthquake victims. The video has had over 201 million views on YouTube.[12]

Sound and music have an enormous capacity to uplift our environment. All music comes from deep within and emerges initially from silence. If the sounds of music have such a profound effect in uniting the different cultures of the world, think of the deeper, profound unifying effect that the experience of the sound of silence would have.

When many people experience the silent music of their souls together at one time, through the group practice of the Transcendental Meditation and advanced TM-Sidhi® programs, the effect can be measured in society as an increase in positive trends. This music for change is "music for world peace," in which every individual participating is a cosmic musician, creating wholeness for themself and the environment.

What Inspired My Book about Enlightenment?

I am often asked the question, "What inspired you to write a book on enlightenment?"[3] I myself am surprised that I wrote a book, especially as I had no intention to do so. I've had the experience of writing many songs, but I'd never even thought about writing a book.

My best songs are those that were totally unplanned and just suddenly and spontaneously bubbled up inside of me; the melody and the words seemed to write themselves. I had the same experience in writing my book *The Transcendental Meditation Technique and the Journey of Enlightenment.*

The whole thing started out so innocently. I wanted to write a short story for my sister as a gift about her singing with our family gardener. After I'd written the first chapter, I thought, "If I'm going to spend a lot of time on this, the content should be more meaningful." As I was peacefully drifting off to sleep that night, a stream of ideas flooded in. I sat up, got a pen and paper, and started writing the ideas down for fear I wouldn't remember them the next morning. This flood of ideas continued almost every night for a month, at which time I had written almost the whole manuscript for a book. A few friends of mine read it and really liked it.

Although the initial writing of the book was easy, the rewriting and editing of it was a challenge. I could not have finished the book without a few excellent editor friends who kindly took the time to make suggestions and review the book several times over.

Every time I felt I hit a roadblock in the rewriting and refining process, when I could not think of a transition paragraph or an introduction to a chapter, I would just completely put the book down. Usually at some point within twenty-four hours the idea that was needed would spontaneously appear in my mind. Knowing that the idea would come was an extremely joyous process for me. I quickly gained the confidence that whatever I needed would bubble up inside me as long as I was easy about it.

Seeing my book published, *The Transcendental Meditation Technique and the Journey of Enlightenment,* gave me a great sense of fulfillment. It's especially thrilling when I hear people say that they love the poems, find it an easy read, and relate to the concepts. My ultimate satisfaction was when my mother said she stayed up all night reading the book!

SECTION 3

HEALTH AND WELL-BEING

Stress: Your Worst Enemy

Due to stress, many of us have endless conversations that go on in our heads and keep us up at night:

"Should I do this or that?"
"I wish I had not said that."
"How do I deal with this difficult person?"
"If only . . ."
And on, and on, and on . . .

Excessive internal dialogue can drive us crazy and become our own worst enemy. I am sure you have heard many times that even if we don't have control over where we are born, who our family is, and many outside circumstances, we still have power over our thoughts and how we play the deck of cards we have been dealt. Easier said than done!

We all want to be kind, loving, diplomatic and harmonious, but when faced with stressful situations, anger or frustration can flare up inside and the internal dialogue goes into full gear.

Your Self: Friend or Foe?

One of my favorite verses in the Bhagavad-Gītā is:

Let a man raise his self by his Self, let him not debase his Self;
he alone, indeed, is his own friend, he alone his own enemy. (6:5)[1]

There are different levels of our self—the active, surface thinking level of our mind, the deeper level of our feelings and intuition, and then the most peaceful level of our being. We can experience this most silent level of our being by transcending through meditation.

The Self Reveals Itself by Itself to Itself

Research on TM[2] shows that when the mind settles down and experiences its own quietest level, the body also gets a very deep state of rest, because the mind and body are interconnected. This deep rest allows stress to be released from the physiology. Your own stress is the unseen enemy[3] that creates disease and also prevents you from being who you really are. When knots or tensions in the physiology start to dissolve, the silent, peaceful nature at the basis of our self is revealed in daily life and overshadowing internal dialogues begin to recede more and more. In activity, we become clearer and more precise in our thinking and are able to achieve what we want more easily. Life takes on a more effortless flow and, as a result, we feel happier.

How Do We Become Our Own Best Friend?

By transcending regularly, we spontaneously feel happier after we meditate—and become more comfortable with our self as a person. We begin to gain mastery of our thoughts and actions as we are no longer caught up and disturbed by agitating or useless thoughts.

This is how we raise our Self by our self. Once we've learned the technique of turning our attention within to the field of pure Being, nothing else from the outside world is needed. We have everything we need inside in order to capture the peaceful qualities latent within the silence of our being. The ocean of calm within our self supports all our activities, regenerates us, gives us energy, nourishes us, soothes us. It is also a field of unconditional love. Who or what could be a better friend?

The World Is as We Are

It is important to understand that meditation does not unfold the self but rather serves as a tool to remove the stress covering our essential nature. In the same way, the wind does nothing to the sun; it only clears away the clouds and allows the sun to shine forth its own light. When the inner light of our being begins to radiate, the world around us also begins to glow.

Arianna Huffington[4] is an advocate of the importance of a good night's rest and has sleep/meditation rooms in her offices because, as she says, sleep is "a performance enhancement tool." She has even started a "Sleep Revolution." Transcendental Meditation provides even deeper rest than sleep, although a good night's sleep is still necessary. Rest is the basis of good health, effectiveness at work, and even the growth of enlightenment.[5]

Enlightenment is the state where we have fully uncovered and realized as a daily reality the inner light ever present in the transcendental silent level of our self. It is so nice to have a best friend whom you can always rely upon. Look no further than yourself.

Social Anxiety Disorder—a Solution

The next time you go to a party, be aware that, according to statistics, one out of every ten people you talk to will be having a severe anxiety[6] attack, be frightened to the core, and be trying desperately to function in that social setting. About 15 million American adults suffer from social anxiety disorder[7]—the third most common disorder after depression and alcoholism.

Causes of Social Anxiety Disorder

The roots of social anxiety disorder[8] can be genetic or biological, and are caused by abnormal functioning of the brain circuits that regulate emotion and the brain's "fight or flight" response. This functioning might be environmentally conditioned, as with children who are overly sheltered at a young age, or psychological, as in the case of a youngster who may have been embarrassed by her teacher or mocked by friends.

We've all felt some degree of nervousness in public, but not usually to the point where it has crippled our behavior. People who have social anxiety disorder depend on what others think of them to feel good. To become free of social anxiety, we have to be comfortable in our own skin. It is easy to say we are comfortable with who we are as a person, but if severe stress or anxiety is present, that comfort will not be experienced.

Our mind is like a computer—our thoughts manifest in our daily life, just as the instructions we give to the computer produce what appears on the screen. There is a verse in the Bhagavad-Gītā: "He who has conquered his self by his Self alone is himself his own friend; but the Self of him who has not conquered his self will behave with enmity like a foe." (6:6)[9]

Treatments for Social Anxiety Disorder

Intense anxiety is enmity that we create in our mind as a response to stress. Drugs may help calm us down and temporarily relieve the anxiety, but they only mask the symptoms. Unfortunately, widespread misuse and overdosing on anti-anxiety drugs[10] has become a major problem in society. These drugs are not a long-term solution. Cognitive Behavioral Therapy (CBT),[11] the most widely used therapy today, teaches people to react differently on an intellectual level to the situations that trigger their anxiety. Often a person will imagine the situation that causes their anxiety and then, in the safety of the therapist's office, work through their fears. However, the underlying stress is still there and can rear its ugly head unexpectedly, at any time.

How can we get rid of stress? The most scientifically validated way to do it is through regular practice of the Transcendental Meditation technique, which allows the mind to settle down to ever quieter levels. Because the mind and body are intimately connected, as the mind settles, so does the body. The body slips into a profound state of rest that allows stress and anxiety to be released.

Veterans suffering from debilitating Post-Traumatic Stress disorder have experienced positive results from TM. In about three months of practicing TM, their symptoms were reduced by 50%.[12] This shows that practicing TM can get rid of both deep-rooted stress as well as day-to-day surface anxiety.

Becoming Our Own Best Friend

Experiencing deeper levels of the mind is soothing to one's well-being. The endless chatter and insecurities that skitter about on the surface of our mind automatically begin to dissolve as we access quieter levels of thought. We feel healed—at peace and whole—ready to tackle the world.

One of the first things I noticed after learning TM was that I felt more at home with myself. I began to care less what other people thought of me because I felt happy and relaxed inside. In time, I even started to feel empowered to do anything I wanted. I had become my own best friend. I felt self-nourished. I stopped constantly getting upset with myself, which had sabotaged the things I attempted to do.

At any time we can be faced with a stressful situation that causes anxiety to bubble up inside us. Although we tell ourselves not to worry, we often can't stifle the endless dialogue and worries running in our minds. When personally faced with this situation, I notice that what seems to be a problem before my regular meditation session is no longer a problem after I finish my meditation. Over time, I have also observed that these stressful external situations don't disrupt my inner well-being as much as they used to.

Everyone should have a best friend with whom they feel supported, nourished, loved, and completely comfortable. Fortunately, you don't have to go anywhere to meet your dearest friend. She is right inside you as your silence. The more you rendezvous with the stillness of your being, the more you will become invincible and able to tackle any storm that blows your way. When you're comfortable with yourself, you can be comfortable in any social situation.

It is not necessary to suffer from the crippling effects of social anxiety disorder. If you dive within to the calm and peace that already exists inside, day-to-day anxiety will gradually dissolve and you'll rise to be an attractive, sparkling light in any social situation.

Enlightened Health Care—Self-Care

I recently read an interesting article called "Top 10 Ways to Put Your Doctor Out of Business"[13] by Dr. Linda Bradley, the Vice Chair of Obstetrics and Gynecology at the Cleveland Clinic in Ohio.

In her article, Dr. Bradley highlights that three out of four people will die of heart disease, diabetes or stroke—three typically self-induced chronic diseases. The article goes on to say that chronic diseases cause 83% of all healthcare spending. These diseases keep our doctors in business, even though most of them can be controlled, or even prevented, through lifestyle changes.

Dr. Bradley suggests that we change our present healthcare system through a SELF-CARE reform. In the article she goes into detail about how heart disease, cancer, diabetes, obesity, etc., can be prevented—mostly through diet and exercise.

Chronic diseases do not appear overnight. Most develop from years of bad eating habits, lack of exercise, and one more item that she did not mention in her article: **stress**. In fact, about 80% of disease is stress-related. The Daily Mail Online reports that:

> Stress has become the most common reason for a worker being signed off long-term sick, a report reveals today. Experts said the psychological condition had become so widespread that it was the '21st century equivalent of the Black Death'. Stress has even eclipsed stroke, heart attack, cancer and back problems, according to the report from the Chartered Institute of Personnel and Development.[14]

The American Heart Association journal, *Circulation: Cardiovascular Quality and Outcomes,* recently published a study showing that African Americans with heart disease who regularly practiced the TM technique were 48% less likely to have a heart attack or stroke, or to die from all other causes, than African Americans who attended a health education class for more than five years.[15]

The research also showed that those practicing Transcendental Meditation lowered their blood pressure and reported less stress and anger. *Time* magazine reported that this is the strongest study yet showing that meditation can lower the risk of heart attack and stroke.[16]

According to Ayurveda, the ancient science of healthcare from India that is rapidly gaining popularity all over the world, all disease initially starts from *Pragyāparādh*—the mistake of the intellect. The mistake of the intellect occurs when we start to identify with everything on the outside, losing the connection with our inner intelligence, the transcendental level of our deepest Self. When we access that inner intelligence in an effortless way through meditation, our mind and body benefit tremendously from the deep rest gained.

This experience of the transcendent, our own pure consciousness, is true "Self-Care." Scientific research on Transcendental Meditation shows benefits in all aspects of life—physiological, psychological, and sociological. Dr. Norman Rosenthal, a prominent psychiatrist, has said that if the benefits to the cardiovascular system of the TM program were available in a pill, "It would be a billion-dollar blockbuster."[17]

By taking ownership of our health, we can be empowered to change our diet, exercise more, and reduce stress in our lives. Our mind is the driver for many of our problems and lack of healthy choices. We can contribute to the overall health of the country simply by creating and securing our own health.

The average American family of four spends almost $25,826 a year in healthcare costs, triple what it was in 2001, according to a 2016 report by Milliman, a global consulting and actuarial firm.[18]

A study published in the September/October 2011 issue of the *American Journal of Health Promotion* showed that people with consistently high healthcare costs experienced a 28% cumulative decrease in physician fees after an average five-year period practicing the Transcendental Meditation technique compared with their baseline.[19] Non-meditating control subjects experienced an increase in fees to physicians over the same time frame.

We have the power to reduce skyrocketing healthcare costs and, more importantly, create true health by turning our present disease-care system into a Self-Care system. As John F. Kennedy so eloquently stated, "Ask not what your country can do for you—ask what you can do for your country."

Transcendental Meditation to Reduce High Blood Pressure

There is great news for the one-in-three Americans who suffer from high blood pressure: You can reduce your blood pressure effectively without medication.

The Wall Street Journal recently highlighted a report titled "Beyond Medications and Diet—Alternative Approaches to Lowering Blood Pressure: A Scientific Statement From the American Heart Association (AHA)." In this report, published April 22, 2013 in the journal *Hypertension*, the American Heart Association concluded that the Transcendental Meditation technique lowers blood pressure and recommends that TM be considered in clinical practice for the prevention and treatment of hypertension.[20]

While there is a significant amount of research on the health benefits of TM, according to researcher Dr. Robert Schneider, this "is the first time TM has been recognized and recommended for consideration by a national medical organization that provides professional practice guidelines to physicians, healthcare providers, and policymakers." The report also states that there is not enough scientific evidence to recommend any other meditation or relaxation techniques.

In 2011, high blood pressure was projected to cost[21] the United States $46.4 billion in health services, medications, and days away from work. High blood pressure is also a cause of strokes and heart attacks, which both add huge costs to our healthcare system. According to another report by the AHA, "Forecasting the Future of Cardiovascular Disease in the United States":

> By 2030, 40.5% of the U.S. population is projected to have some form of CVD [cardiovascular disease]. Between 2010 and 2030, real total direct medical costs of CVD are projected to triple, from $273 billion to $818 billion. Real indirect costs (due to lost

productivity) for all CVD are estimated to increase from $172 billion in 2010 to $276 billion in 2030, an increase of 61%.[22]

If the TM practice can help reduce high blood pressure, and even prevent it in the first place, this cost-effective approach could save our country billions of dollars.[23]

As mentioned in a previous blog, research has been conducted in over 250 independent research institutes worldwide, with the American National Institutes of Health[24] funding over $26 million of research on the health benefits of Transcendental Meditation. Research shows improved heart health,[25] reduced anxiety and stress,[26] improved memory and learning ability,[27] increased creativity[28] and emotional stamina, reversal of aging[29] and many other benefits from the simple practice of Transcendental Meditation. Health insurance companies want to save money, the government wants to reduce our national budget, taxpayers want to pay less taxes, and everyone wants to be healthy! Many who take high blood pressure medication do not like the side-effects that come with it. Introducing Transcendental Meditation into our healthcare system is a win, win, win, win situation. This is true healthcare—Self-care[30]—first preventing disease,[31] and, secondly, treating disease in a natural and cost-effective way.[32]

Now that the support of the AHA has been added to the already ample body of evidence on the impact of Transcendental Meditation in reducing high blood pressure, what are we waiting for? Let's move full speed ahead and demand that insurance companies, Medicare, and Medicaid pay for the cost of learning Transcendental Meditation, in the same way they cover other complementary and alternative medical arts such as acupuncture, massage therapy, holistic psychotherapy, stress management techniques, yoga therapies, and chiropractic care.

In one stroke, no pun intended, we can address the problems of skyrocketing healthcare costs, and more importantly, stem the tide of ill health that currently envelops our population. As individual health improves, societal consciousness will naturally rise and we will all enjoy living in a more successful, enlightened society.

A Heavenly Haven for Health and Enlightenment

I recently spent a deeply nourishing time in the cornfields of Iowa at The Raj—an Ayurveda health spa.[33] Beneath beautiful skies and amid the vast farmlands of Fairfield, Iowa, down a road graced with the most vibrant, colorful leaves of pear trees I have ever seen, stands a charming building reminiscent of the French countryside. Walking in through the doors, I immediately felt vibrant silence and my physiology began to unwind from the frenetic activity of the world.

The Raj is the most authentic Ayurveda health spa in America. Ayurveda,[34] which literally means knowledge of life span, or immortality, is an ancient science of healthcare from India that focuses mainly on prevention and also eliminates disease through natural means.

The Royal Treatment

I couldn't wait to start the treatments, which are individually tailored to the patient's needs and are determined on arrival after meeting with the doctor. Being bathed in warm soothing oils by two highly trained technicians made me feel like a queen. Each day I felt more relaxed as I easily sunk into each luxurious session. My favorite treatment is called *shirodhara*, which consists of warm herbalized oil that is gently poured back and forth on the forehead, for about twenty to thirty minutes. The warm oil flowing on my forehead stilled the barrage of thoughts that were going through my mind.

The organic food was delicious, and I never felt cravings for any other food, like my usual daily dose of chocolate. Yoga asanas kept my body flexible and light. Daily walks soothed my senses on the outer level of beauty. The knowledge lectures in the evening were also extremely stimulating, keeping my intellect engaged and satisfied.

A Maharishi Vāstu®—Sthāpatya Veda—Hotel

The Raj hotel is built according to principles of Maharishi Vāstu®,[35] based on the ancient science of architecture also from India that offers guidelines for constructing buildings and homes according to natural law. Just being in the building, with the lovely soft decor and artwork, was uplifting to the senses. The symmetric design created a feeling of orderliness. I loved waking up every morning with the sun pouring into my room, and felt the building itself was sparkling with lively consciousness.

A Quantum Leap

During my stay at The Raj my meditations took a quantum leap in clarity. I can even say divinity, as the sparkling qualities of pure consciousness zoomed forth in my awareness, bestowing moments of pure bliss.

Every day I felt such gratitude for being able to come and receive a week of treatment. By the end of my stay I felt refreshed, clear, and energized. Another couple also going through the treatment while I was there said that they used to go away on vacation to luxurious, well-known resorts. Now they want to spend their vacation time at The Raj once a year, because afterwards they feel more rejuvenated and renewed than from any other vacation they have taken.

If you want an ideal vacation—to enjoy a time of rest and rejuvenation—The Raj is one of the best places to visit.

SECTION 4

ENLIGHTENMENT

The Journey of Enlightenment— You Don't Need to Go Anywhere

To change the trajectory of your life in a big way, you probably think you have to drop whatever you are doing to make a complete change. Like Elizabeth Gilbert, author of *Eat, Pray, Love*, you pack your bags and head off to an ashram in India. You may decide to go to a Buddhist monastery, to a yoga retreat in Costa Rica, or to visit sacred places like Machu Picchu in Peru. You could even go on a long hike like Cheryl Strayed,[1] who wrote the book *Wild: From Lost To Found on the Pacific Crest Trail*. Strayed writes that she was hoping for a transformational experience that would "make me into the woman I knew I could become and turn me back into the girl I'd once been." On your journey, you take time for inner reflection, meditate at these sacred places, walk in nature, and hopefully come back with a renewed vision of life and the answers to your questions. However, many people are not in a position to suddenly drop everything and take a soul-searching trip to some far-off land.

All Seekers Find Their Answers Within

Fortunately, to answer the big questions of life or to begin the journey of inner enlightenment you do not have to travel anywhere. The ironic lesson all these searchers realize is that the answers to their questions and fulfillment lie directly inside them.

The journey of enlightenment begins not by going anywhere, but by unfolding what already exists within. At the depth of the heart and mind of every person on this planet is an unbounded oasis of calm, peace, love, and bliss. This state is the transcendental level of our Being. It is the most silent level of our consciousness.

Tap into the Transcendent

We just need to tap into this level through meditation and day-by-day the evolutionary qualities of the transcendent will blossom in our daily life. When we hear the word meditation, many of us may think, "There is no way I can sit still for even one second!" I genuinely felt sorry for Elizabeth Gilbert as her beginning days of meditating seemed excruciatingly difficult. Fortunately, after several weeks in the ashram, she did have some positive experiences.

I was fortunate to learn the Transcendental Meditation[2] technique as taught by Maharishi Mahesh Yogi[3] in 1972. Right from my first meditation, I settled down in a natural and effortless way to the most peaceful silence I had ever experienced.

Without ever having thought about the possibility of enlightenment, after my first meditation I knew my journey of enlightenment had begun. Experiencing the transcendent within was so profound that it unexpectedly changed the trajectory of my life 180 degrees—without my having to go anywhere.

The Self Unfolds Itself, to Itself, by Itself, within Itself, for Itself

Enlightenment is the full blossoming of the transcendental, cosmic universal value of our Self, along with the development of the full potential of our unique individual values.

Just by taking twenty minutes twice a day to experience this expanded, silent level of ourselves, we can come out of meditation feeling refreshed, renewed, and with a broader vision of life. All the qualities of the transcendent—peace, calm, love, fullness, and an unbounded state of awareness—grow naturally day by day in whatever we are doing in our lives.

Getting away from your usual surroundings may give you a fresh perspective on, and temporary relief from, whatever you are going through in your life. Certainly, just getting away for some rest and relaxation helps you to feel renewed and refreshed—until the daily grind back home quickly overtakes you again.

Start your journey of enlightenment now by embarking on a first-class journey to the ultimate place of luxury—the pure silence of your soul. Travel the royal road to the boundlessly joyful state of your being, which will suffuse freedom to all the boundaries of your life. Walk the pathless path through the doors of your cosmic dwelling and live in that house forever!

Take Only One Road

There are many roads to take,
many directions to go,
many skies to fly,
many oceans to row.

There are many hills to climb,
many paths to follow,
many rivers to cross,
but their ends are shallow.

Take only one path—
one joyous road,
let all travel converge into Self's heavenly abode.

Let go of outer direction,
let Self be your guiding hand—
the purpose of any journey
is to end in God's land.

You will end up there
after many mountains crossed,
cut short your long journey
on useless paths getting lost.

The way is simple, effortless—
faster than a jet plane.
Let your compass point you within
to Heaven's domain.

Never swerve from your path—always stay right on course.
You will arrive in a flash,
in heaven, your own silent source.

Enlightenment: The Missing Element

In my upbringing, there was never any discussion about enlightenment, period. I had never heard of enlightenment as a possibility in any church service, or any educational program. Even in India the concept of enlightenment is reserved for the rare few recluses who wish to live in a cave or wander on foot and give up all worldly possessions.

I have learned that, just as a flower's natural tendency is to bloom and blossom, enlightenment is the most natural state of the human nervous system, which has immense practical value for day-to-day life. It is the missing and most essential element for the benefit of society.

What Is Enlightenment?

Enlightenment is becoming the person you are meant to be. For me it means enjoying 24 hours of inner and outer peace and contentment. Here is how Maharishi Mahesh Yogi, the founder of the Transcendental Meditation program, defines enlightenment:

> Enlightenment is the state of consciousness, which is always evolutionary, progressive—never negative and never defeated. Once one is in light, one doesn't tumble as one does in darkness . . . That's how we would define enlightenment—a lively state of all possibilities, a state of no failure, no weakness, no problems, no suffering—that kind of state of consciousness, that kind of state of life.[4]

This may sound like an out-of-reach fanciful idea, especially if you were taught like I was that it is necessary to struggle in life. The closest teaching to enlightenment I received was that if I lived a good moral life, I might make it to heaven afterwards. Waiting until the afterlife for a promise of heaven with no proof that it could be fulfilled was not an option for me.

Discover the Field of Silence and Peace Within

Although I would not change any of the important lessons learned during my teenage years, meditating earlier on in life would have saved me from a lot of stress. I know I would have been a more focused student. I wonder if I had attention-deficit disorder (ADD) during high school. I always had a hard time focusing in class and during my summer jobs.

The day I learned to meditate I was 18 years old. My life took an unexpected turn as I discovered a field of silence, peace, and bliss inside. Outwardly, there was a deepening experience of contentment, energy, efficiency, and focus. I now had the ability to focus in on my schoolwork, and to choose more life-supporting behaviors. There was an inner stability growing in me; I was less upset by outside circumstances. Becoming more focused in every undertaking was one of the first benefits I noticed from learning to meditate.

Enlightenment: Our Birthright

Maharishi said from his earliest days of teaching Transcendental Meditation that enlightenment is our birthright; and the goal of all life is to develop the full potential of who we are.

I firmly believe that it is essential for students to start meditating in school[5] at about ten years of age. By meditating earlier on, children tend to be happier and more grounded. These students will be more likely to see how, on a deeper level, all of life is interconnected. They will have a vision of the whole range of life, from the depths of their silent being to the outer changing values of daily life. With this understanding, our children will create industries more beneficial to the environment and the well-being of all people. They will also have a broadened awareness to help bring urgently needed solutions to the issues now facing our world.

The fundamental solutions we need to change the world exist right here, inside of everyone. How could we have missed this essential element? We have been looking in the wrong direction: outside. It is time now to open our eyes (and by open I mean close) and embrace the light that shines within each of us. This light is the silent transcendental level of our own Being, and is experienced by transcending.

As Jackie DeShannon says in her song, "What the World Needs Now is Love, Sweet Love."[6] That love is inside us, waiting for its power to be unleashed to unify and bring peace to the world. Let's not miss this most essential element in a child's upbringing, and at any stage of human life.

The Journey of Enlightenment

There are many concepts of enlightenment. Maharishi Mahesh Yogi described enlightenment as a state of consciousness whereby one is content and feels fulfilled twenty-four hours a day, independent of outside circumstances. Even if something bad happens on the outside, the person may still experience momentary sadness, but the emotion does not overshadow the underlying, stable inner happiness. In addition, enlightenment means living one's full mental potential, and being in harmony with natural law.

A Mother Cultures Her Child's Enlightenment

The transference of a mother's love[7] and joy to her baby cultures the child to become strong and happy, which nurtures the growth of enlightenment. Children are like a sponge absorbing everything from their environment. The more love and support they receive, the more they will grow to be integrated citizens able to contribute to the well-being of society. If a child does not receive the love and attention he needs, he may experience many problems as he matures into adulthood.

Does Education Develop Our Full Potential?

Education should further the growth of one's well-being and potential; its aim is to develop a fully rounded, integrated, happy human being. However, during the educational years many situations can restrict the growth of our mental potential. These include stress, drugs, alcohol abuse, and an education that does not inspire or satisfy the student's thirst for knowledge.

Unfortunately, an epidemic of stress pervades the daily life of college students, resulting in the widespread use of drugs, prescription pills and alcohol. Neurological imaging research[8] shows that drug addiction can create "functional holes" in the brain—areas of the cortex which do not receive blood flow and thus remain unengaged in the task at hand, whether it be decision making, judgment, or planning.

Meditation Increases Brain Functioning

Research on meditation,[9] particularly Transcendental Meditation (TM), shows an increase in one's brain functioning,[10] and shows higher levels of coherence in the prefrontal cortex during transcendence. Research also shows that practice of TM significantly reduces stress levels.[11] If we introduce meditation to students in schools at an early age, around ten years old, we can help them grow up with significantly less stress, while at the same time improving their ability to focus and learn.[12]

Education for Enlightenment

Enlightenment should no longer be considered a foreign, impractical concept. It is the birthright of everyone to be happy, healthy, and living full potential—life in higher states of consciousness. Anything less should be considered abnormal.

Education can and should be a journey of enlightenment whereby students graduate happy, healthy, and with the ability to use their full mental capacity. If we allow students to graduate without reaching their potential, then we cannot expect them to be balanced individuals able to come up with holistic solutions to the many urgent problems facing our world today. These problems are caused in part by shortsighted thinkers who do not have the broad comprehension necessary to see the effect of their actions on society as a whole. Through the process of transcending, you open your awareness to the whole range of the mind. Just as importantly, the ocean of inner happiness fills your Being, and the wisdom of silence starts to steer you through life in a more harmonious, productive way.

Transcendence—the Gateway to Enlightenment

Lao Tzu said, "The journey of a thousand miles begins with one step." The journey of enlightenment really begins when you dive within and experience the silent depths of your mind.

Maharishi Mahesh Yogi has described seven states of consciousness. We are all familiar with the first three, waking, dreaming, and sleeping—that we experience in our day-to-day lives. The fourth state, transcendental consciousness, has unique physiological parameters and is the basis and gateway for unfolding the other higher states of consciousness.

Everyone should enjoy the light of his or her fully awakened consciousness within. This most natural state fulfills the purpose of life—to become the fully blossomed flower you are meant to be!

Fully Blossomed

My breath has become breathless
as I merge with the stillness of the gentle hour—
the holy time is hovering everywhere
my heart no longer beats yet has a power
of purest love flowing here and there.
I feel fully blossomed like a flower
dancing in the evening air.
The universe, my soul, my mind
are one harmonious song that shares
the sweetness—the rhythm beyond all time.

Are You Living Only Three of the Seven States of Consciousness?

In our quiet moments, we often ask ourselves the question, "Is there more to life?" or "What is the purpose of my life?" In the search for more meaning, we tend to explore different activities. We try to meet new people. Maybe we find a new and satisfying job, eventually get married, join a book club, go to a yoga class or the gym, take up a musical instrument or new sport, or go on a trip. The list goes on and on.

Three Common States of Consciousness

We live our 24/7 daily cycles of life by going through the waking, dreaming, and sleeping states of consciousness—that is, unless we have perpetual insomnia!

The waking state of consciousness offers endless possibilities for enjoyment, but the outside world is always changing, so the pleasure or satisfaction that comes with these new additions to our life is only temporary.

The sleeping state of consciousness provides deep rest and is well-known to be essential for our survival. Sleep serves to rejuvenate the mind and prepare the physiology to meet the next day's challenges. Without the deep rest of sleep, our body cannot function effectively in daily life.

The dreaming state, also called Rapid Eye Movement (REM) sleep, is necessary to release stress accumulated during the day and thereby revitalize the mind. Research has shown that the REM state stimulates regions of the brain used for learning, memory, and filing of past impressions for future use.

Transcendental Consciousness— a Fourth State of Consciousness

There is a fourth major state of consciousness[13] that scientists have documented as being distinct from waking, dreaming, and sleeping— transcendental consciousness. In 1970, in the popular journal *Science*,

Dr. Robert Keith Wallace published a groundbreaking study entitled "Physiological Effects of Transcendental Meditation."[14]

His research showed that the experience of transcendental consciousness during Transcendental Meditation produced a profound state of rest, deeper even than sleep, as seen by greatly reduced oxygen consumption. The research also showed significant decreases in breathing and heart rate, as well as indicators of deep relaxation, normalization of blood pressure, and a state of restful alertness, as measured by EEG changes in the alpha and theta wave activity. Dr. Wallace concluded that these markedly distinct physiological changes indicate a fourth major state of consciousness.

To date, there is an extensive body of peer-reviewed studies[15] published on Transcendental Meditation that indicate the benefits of experiencing this fourth state of consciousness—transcendental consciousness. This research points to improvements on all levels of life—psychological, physiological, and sociological.

Cosmic Consciousness

Maharishi Mahesh Yogi, who brought Transcendental Meditation to the West, has explained that transcendental consciousness serves as a bridge to three "higher" states of consciousness—cosmic consciousness,[16] glorified cosmic consciousness, and unity consciousness.

Cosmic consciousness results from gradual release of stress over time due to the deep rest gained during TM. Eventually the nervous system becomes stress free and is able to maintain the state of transcendental consciousness even during dynamic activity. All the sublime qualities of the transcendent that one accesses during the twenty minutes twice daily practice of Transcendental Meditation—silence, profound peace, unbounded awareness—become a continuum of our daily life. This silence even continues during deep sleep and dreaming! These qualities and many health benefits develop naturally over time through the regular practice of Transcendental Meditation.

In his classic book, *Science of Being and Art of Living*, Maharishi declared:

> Cosmic consciousness should not be considered as something far beyond the reach of normal man. The state of cosmic consciousness should be the state of normal human consciousness. Any state below cosmic consciousness can only be taken to be subnormal human consciousness. The human mind should be a cosmically conscious mind.[17]

Glorified Cosmic Consciousness

Established in cosmic consciousness, one has gained a permanent state of finer stability and freedom, a state of complete independence from the ever-changing, ephemeral field of life. From this state of true liberation, we are in a position to enjoy the whole sensory range of life without being overwhelmed by its ever-changing nature. In cosmic consciousness, even though our mind and senses have become free from stress, there is still more delightful evolution that awaits us. As we continue to transcend through our TM practice, our senses refine further, and we start to experience more delicate, hitherto unperceived, levels of the objects of our experience.

Long before the state of cosmic consciousness has been permanently established, signposts on the way to the glorified state of cosmic consciousness crop up. A common experience that people report after learning Transcendental Meditation is that the beauty and details of their surroundings are felt and experienced more intimately. This deeper appreciation of the surroundings causes their hearts to open more and to flow in gratitude toward their environment, including to family and friends. This warm flow in the state of contentment is simply called love!

Unity Consciousness

The steady, limitless flow of love from within the heart that develops in glorified cosmic consciousness is like a river that connects inner and outer. It is also like a cup overflowing. The qualities of pure consciousness flow out through all our faculties in love and gratitude. The inner experience of infinity in transcendental consciousness is reflected out through the senses, creating an experience of unity consciousness, where one's inner, unbounded bliss consciousness is perceived pulsating in the environment.

Many people throughout the ages have reported experiences of unity consciousness. An excerpt from *The Over-Soul,* an essay by Ralph Waldo Emerson[18] published in 1841, expresses this reality:

> . . . within man is the soul of the whole, the wise silence, the universal beauty to which every part and particle is equally related; the eternal One. And this deep power in which we exist, and whose beatitude is all accessible to us, is not only self-sufficing and perfect in every hour, but the act of seeing and the thing seen, the seer and the spectacle, the subject and the object, are one. We see the world piece by piece, as the sun, the moon, the animal, the tree; but the whole, of which these are the shining parts, is the soul . . .[19]

Writers, artists, scientists, athletes—people from all backgrounds—have reported experiences of higher states of consciousness that happened spontaneously at some point during their lives. These experiences were so profound that they transformed the trajectory of their lives. However, often these people expressed frustration at being unable to repeat the experience. Moreover, without an intellectual framework to understand their experience, many spent the remainder of their lives doubting or despairing over ever having such an experience again.

Fortunately today, through the regular practice of Transcendental Meditation, we can grow in higher states of consciousness in a natural, spontaneous way. Maharishi has made thousands of hours of fascinating tapes giving in-depth explanations about transcendental consciousness, cosmic consciousness, glorified cosmic consciousness, and unity consciousness. Many of these videotaped lectures by Maharishi on higher states of consciousness can be viewed at Transcendental Meditation centers worldwide. There are also videos available of Maharishi on YouTube.[20]

During quiet moments, when we think "there has to be more to life," if we search only in the waking state of consciousness for that "more," we will never find true and lasting fulfillment. Right from birth, you have been evolving into the person you are meant to become. Journeying to the silence of your mind and passing through the gate into transcendental consciousness, you will start to unfold your cosmic potential. The sooner you can start on this journey, the more you will enjoy the beauty of the path of growing enlightenment in every breath of your life.

Rather than restricting your life to only the waking, dreaming, and sleeping states of consciousness, take a dive within to begin enjoying the limitless, blissful state of unity consciousness and become the whole person who you are truly meant to be.

Enlightenment: More than Just a State of Mind

When it comes to enlightenment and personal development today, most spiritual teachings tend to put the cart before the horse. They approach changing one's life on the level of the *intellect*—through changing one's attitudes, trying to be present or mindful of the moment, trying to get beyond one's ego, etc.

Changing your thinking does have positive benefits. However, the difficulty of this approach is that it does not inherently develop higher states of consciousness. Enlightenment is not a *mood* of being happy or being present. It is based on profound neurophysiological changes that allow the mind and body to live in a continuous state of complete integration—free from stress and strain.

We know stress is a major factor in many diseases. In fact, 80% of disease today is stress-related. If we are really stressed or unhappy we can try to mentally snap out of our depression, but even if we succeed in doing so we are not necessarily releasing the underlying stress that caused the sadness.

Meditation for Enlightenment

How does meditation change the physiology? Research on Transcendental Meditation specifically shows that when the mind settles down to a state of restful alertness—pure consciousness—the breath rate settles down too, as indicated by decreased oxygen consumption.[21] This profound state of deep rest allows the body to eliminate accumulated stress and anxiety.

Research also shows increased brain wave coherence[22] even from one's very first meditation. As a result, one becomes naturally more present, more fulfilled, happier, less bothered by the ups and downs of life. This is growing *enlightenment*—a physiological state of coherence, balance, and integration that can be scientifically measured.[23]

Research on Meditation Techniques

There are striking differences in the physiological effects of various meditation techniques.[24] Unfortunately, many journalists and teachers of meditation tend to lump the extensive research on meditation into one body of generic research. For example, there are many different types of mindfulness meditation, but research has only been conducted on a few kinds.

There are over 360 studies on Transcendental Meditation published in peer-reviewed journals,[25] and because Transcendental Meditation is taught in exactly the same systematic way in every part of the world, it makes research on TM more pristine and rigorous, since every practitioner undergoes the same instructional process.

Finding the Right Meditation for You

When looking for a technique of meditation, it is worthwhile to investigate the relevant scientific research and make sure it relates to the technique you are learning. If you are contemplating a technique that just promotes positive thinking, know that for what it is—trying to change yourself through an intellectual approach that may not transform your physiology.

Most of all, make sure that the technique is easy and natural. After all, the reason you want to meditate in the first place is to feel happier and healthier in your life!

SECTION 5

BLISS AND SILENCE

Bliss—Our Essential Nature

Out of bliss, all beings are born,
In bliss they are sustained,
And to bliss they go and merge again.

Ānandāddhyeva khalvimāni bhūtāni jāyante
ānandena jātāni jīvanti
ānandaṃ prayantyabhisaṃvishanti

—Taittirīya Upanishad (3.6.1)[1]

This verse about bliss is my favorite quote from the Vedic Literature, the ancient wisdom cognized by seers in India and explained by Maharishi. One time my sister said to me, "why do you always use the word *bliss*?" It made me realize that most people can relate to being happy, but few people can relate to bliss as the reality of their daily life. If bliss is the source, nature, and ultimate goal of life, why isn't it a common experience?

The Difference between Bliss and Happiness

Most people have experiences of happiness, at least some of the time. Happiness is a state of well-being or contentment. What is the difference between happiness and bliss? Bliss can be defined as more than just a fleeting moment of happiness. It is an experience of wholeness, complete happiness, heavenly joy, and, in its most stabilized form, the state of enlightenment.

Two Realities of Life

There are two realities of life, the outer and the inner. In our day-to-day outer activities the experience of bliss can be hidden, just like the fluid property of water is hidden when it is ice. Our mind and senses are so accustomed to experiencing only outer objects and situations that the inner experience of latent, transcendental bliss is easily missed.

Most people experience happiness as a result of an outside pleasurable situation—the birth of a child, being with friends, walking in nature, enjoying a party, or if you are my brother, having a good game of golf. Actually, according to him, golf might fall into the *bliss* category.

When the mind begins to experience finer regions of thought through techniques like Transcendental Meditation, and eventually transcends even the finest level of thought, it will experience the state of pure bliss—its own essential nature. Gaining familiarity with our inner bliss allows us to recognize bliss in our surroundings, because our inner state determines how we experience the world outside of us.

Cranky and grumpy? The world looks gray, and we feel beset by obstacles and problems. Happy and content? The world seems bright and full of promise. The world is as we are. With regular practice of TM, very naturally and effortlessly we gradually develop a state of inner bliss that does not depend on anything from the outside. At the same time, our inner joy and contentment infuses the activities of our lives with positivity, confidence, and a profound sense of stability and well-being, ultimately leading to the beautiful goal of full enlightenment, in which bliss is the outer and the inner reality.

Why Suffer?

Many people feel suffering is a natural part of life. If you are not anchored to the silent, transcendental value of your Being, it certainly is! You can easily be tossed about and upset by the constant winds of changing circumstances—your life is like an unanchored boat at the mercy of the sea. You are inevitably vulnerable to disappointment and to suffering as things you love come and go. In contrast, the path of bliss within is straight, easy, effortless, and open to everyone because it is the essential nature of everyone. Why suffer or settle for only moments of happiness when we can enjoy our essential nature—peaceful inner stability and bliss?

Follow Your Bliss

"Follow your bliss" was a phrase promoted by the renowned mythologist and author Joseph Campbell.[2] As he said: "I feel that if one follows what I call one's bliss—the thing that really gets you deep in the gut that you feel is your life—doors will open up. They do!"[3]

Campbell is essentially advising us to listen to our inner voice deep within—that will steer us in a more positive direction and the wonderful things will start to happen. The thing I find most interesting about this comment is that he is saying: go within—feel what is inside.

Bliss: Our Essential Nature

Maharishi Mahesh Yogi has described that our own essential nature is in reality a state of bliss. He often quoted a Sanskrit expression that explains consciousness as *sat, chit, ānanda.*

Sat means the absolute, non-changing reality of life.

Chit means consciousness, or wakefulness.

Ānanda means bliss.

Enlightenment is just waking up to, or becoming aware of, this inner reality of pure bliss.

Bliss: The Message of All the Great Teachers

Maharishi brought Transcendental Meditation out of the Himalayas to bring this concrete experience of bliss to the world. He often said that "the purpose of life is the expansion of happiness" and that "life is here to enjoy." When we experience our essential nature through meditation, this reality of bliss grows more and more as a state of Being not dependent on anything from the outside for its fulfillment. All the great teachers throughout time have expounded this reality.

It amazes me to think that within every one of the seven billion people on this planet lies this state of absolute bliss. Yet, unfortunately, relatively few people access it, or are even aware of it. In recent years, however, a spiritual awakening is clearly taking place and more and more people are becoming aware of this transcendental reality. Just imagine how transformed the world would be if all people were enjoying endless inner bliss, instead of being bogged down with stress, strain, and ill-health.

Bliss Is Not a Mood

The reality of bliss within is not just a nice, fanciful New Age idea. It is not a mood, or an attitude, of happiness. In fact, trying to be happy can even create strain, especially if you are actually feeling bad. Also, trying to be happy or positive can foster an insincere and disingenuous state of mind—mood-making—which can be bothersome to those around. Have you ever been around someone who is pretending to be happy? It is so easy to see right through them.

Can Bliss Be Measured?

When we are feeling well, we naturally feel happier. Since bliss is our own fundamental nature, by reducing stress we simply create a situation for bliss to spontaneously blossom. The extensive amount of scientific research showing that the practice of Transcendental Meditation significantly reduces stress in the physiology explains why practitioners of TM also report markedly increased happiness in their lives.

Studies have shown:[4]

- Decreased depression
- Reduced coronary heart disease
- Decreased stress
- Increased Self-Confidence and Self-Actualization
- Orientation towards positive values

Although we want to follow our bliss in the outside world, as advised by Joseph Campbell, the outside world is always changing and those moments of happiness will always be fleeting. Bliss is more than just a momentary experience of happiness in the outer world. It is a transcendental experience of wholeness, complete happiness, heavenly joy, and, in its most stabilized form, a continuum of bliss is a hallmark of the state of enlightenment.

Bliss Is Not an Attitude

Many people try to be happy. Although well-intentioned and sincere in their efforts, it usually does not work. Trying to create happiness by pretending to feel it is not sustainable and can even create strain and headache, especially if one actually feels bad but is pretending to feel wonderful.

Trying to invoke some feeling of bliss when one is interacting socially may foster an insincere approach to communicating. "Oh, I feel so blissful and everything is just marvelous," when it actually is not, is making a sham of one's inner truth. Summoning a blissful mood and trying to maintain it while engaged in activity is not healthy for our natural flow of emotions. Indeed, if our purpose in mood-making is to try to impress other people, we are defeating ourselves, because most people will sense the artificiality and will tend to be put off.

I am certainly not speaking badly of someone who is trying to change his or her mood by thinking positively. It is good to have a positive attitude. If one is feeling disillusioned or depressed, rallying one's confidence and focusing on the good in the situation rather than the bad is entirely helpful. However, keep a truthful vision of yourself and your situation and do not impose a fake smile or unreal pretensions of some kind or another. It is ok to just be what you are. But what are we, really?

Bliss: A Byproduct of Diving Within

In each one of us there is a field of bliss, which we can access. It is a field of true and lasting peace. According to the Vedas, all of creation is ultimately made of bliss. This is what we are at our core. This is what we want to infuse, like a rare perfume, into all facets of our existence.

Bliss: The Message of All Great Teachers

When we experience our essential nature through meditation, this reality of bliss grows more and more as a state of Being. This inner experience of Being is not dependent on anything from the outside for its fulfillment. All the great teachers throughout time have expounded the reality of inner bliss.

Bliss—Unchanging in a Changing World

The outside world is always changing and moments of happiness will always go as quickly as they come. The bliss I am speaking of here is more than just a momentary experience of happiness in the outer world. It is a transcendental experience of wholeness, complete happiness, contentment, and heavenly joy. In its most stabilized form the continuum of bliss is a hallmark of the state of enlightenment.

Traveling to experience this bliss within is the first step on the journey toward enlightenment. The most beautiful aspect of this journey is that you don't have to go anywhere. The Self unfolds itself, to itself, by itself, within itself, for itself. By enjoying the bliss within you can naturally and spontaneously live bliss more and more in everyday life.

It is so much easier to be who you are than trying to be something or someone else!

The Silence Revolution

Recently, I read a Huffington Post article about the "Quiet Revolution,"[5] a notion proposed by Susan Cain, author of the book *Quiet: The Power of Introverts in a World That Can't Stop Talking*. In fact, Huffington Post has joined forces[6] with this laudable revolution. The purpose of the Quiet Revolution is to inspire introverts to express their convictions, talents, and passions within today's boisterous world of overpowering extroverts.

I propose taking the revolution one step deeper—from quiet to silence—to a "Silence Revolution."

What Is a Silence Revolution?

At first, it may seem odd to put the words Silence and Revolution together. How does a "Silence Revolution" work?

Fulfillment is based on successful action. Effective action is based on powerful, comprehensive thinking. A powerful thought force is based on inner silence, just as the most powerful ocean waves arise from a swell in the ocean's depths. The more we experience the state of silence in the depths of our being—the place from where all thoughts originate and take shape—the more successful we will be in our undertakings, whether we are an introvert or an extrovert.

Every person on earth has a field of silence within. Innate to the ability to run is the ability to walk, and the ability to walk contains the ability to stand still. It is the same with the mind. Inherent in the ability to talk is the ability to think; the ability to think contains the ability to think quietly—to feel or intuit. The ability to think quietly holds the possibility for the mind to be completely still.

Silence is the natural ground state of our being and is the most powerful level of the mind. As we come closer to a light bulb, the light becomes stronger and brighter. In the same way, our most powerful thoughts are those that are consciously projected from their source, the field of silent awareness.

How to Experience Silence

Yoga postures and exercises, also known as *asanas*, are one way that people experience silence and transformation. *Asanas* are important for building a strong and flexible physiology and offer many health benefits. They are an effective way to calm and refresh the mind. There can be moments within a yoga session when the mind may become deeply settled.

However, meditation can be far more effective than yoga *asanas* for experiencing the state of pure silence. There is a difference between the relaxation gained in the average physical yoga practice and the inward experience of deep silence during transcendence, which is a fourth major state of consciousness.[7]

The type of meditation I have found to be most profound for clearly experiencing the state of pure silence is Transcendental Meditation. What I like about TM is that it is completely natural and effortless; it allows me to transcend the surface level of the mind. I experience finer and finer thoughts until even the finest thought impulse is transcended and my awareness opens to the state of transcendence—pure silence—Being.

This total settling of the mind has innumerable health benefits. Because the mind and body are intimately connected, as the mind goes to quieter levels during Transcendental Meditation, the body naturally settles into a profound state of rest. This deep rest allows blockages and imbalances in the body to dissolve. As the physiological systems are healed and repaired, they function more effectively.

During the practice of Transcendental Meditation the brain produces high-power alpha waves.[8] This distinct brain pattern corresponds to a state of restful alertness—inner wakefulness characterized by serenity, expanded awareness and bliss. Additionally, the alpha waves become synchronous, rising and falling together. This coherence of alpha waves often spreads throughout the brain and is strongest in the prefrontal cortex—the seat of your brain's executive judgment.

The practice of TM also creates coherence between the left and right brain hemispheres.[9] Such holistic brain functioning results in improved mental performance—better memory, increased creativity, broader comprehension, and sharper mental focus. Over time, the coherent brain functioning found during the practice of TM when eyes are closed is seen when the eyes are open—the improved functioning becomes stabilized outside of meditation.[10]

For decades, psychology has suggested we are not using our full mental potential. If this is so, how can we expect a partially developed mind to create anything more than partially developed solutions to problems?

Scientific research clearly indicates that when we give students the opportunity to learn Transcendental Meditation, the result is a greater use of mental potential.[11] A new generation of bright, resourceful, happy individuals will face humanity's age-old challenges, and apply more human potential than has yet been available to come up with holistic, far-reaching solutions.

We All Want a Revolution

Age after age, the cry for change in the world has continued, and never more so than today. Revolution has become a buzzword in the media. Comedian Russell Brand's book *Revolution* echoes countless others in saying that our political and social systems are basically dysfunctional, our values topsy-turvy, and our lives lacking something essential. Bernie Sanders has been calling for a political revolution for decades. The surprising momentum Mr. Sanders gained during the 2016 presidential campaign is yet another sign that many Americans desire change, even a revolution—a truly deep transformation.

Water the Root to Enjoy the Fruit

In our ever-evolving world, various kinds of revolution are inevitable, and some can lead to positive outcomes. If we wish to transform all the surface values of life in one fell swoop for the betterment of all, we must attend to their foundation. Like a gardener who waters the root of a tree to supply nourishment to all its branches, leaves, flowers and fruits, we must attend to the root of our existence by nourishing and infusing all aspects of life with the innermost peace and power of the lively vibrant silence at the source of thought. Introverts will become stronger in themselves and enjoy expressing themselves more; extroverts may settle down and respectfully listen to introverts. If enough people experience this most natural state of calm coherence within, we could generate a powerful influence of peace in the world.[12] How about we "give peace a chance"? Join the millions around the world already engaged in a Silence Revolution to create peace from the level of peace within.

The Power of Silence

The most silent time of year in nature is January and February, at least in the northern hemisphere. Walking outside on a snowy day, there are no sounds of birds singing through the air, no rustling of leaves whispering in the wind, even rivers and lakes are immovable, frozen into tranquility. All around everything is still except the silent falling of snow.

Have you ever thought about the power of silence? Maharishi Mahesh Yogi began every new year with a week of silence. When the week was over he would emerge with an incredible dynamism of new ideas and plans for the coming year.

Unseen Talents of Silence

An Ayurvedic doctor once said to me: always be respectful of people who seem more quiet and introverted because usually they have some unique talent or skill that they have cultured quietly by themselves.

Our success in life is based on our actions, our actions are based on our thoughts, and our thoughts are based on our being—a field of pure silence. The more we are grounded in that silence, the stronger our base will be; the more powerful our actions will be, the greater our success and fulfillment.

Like a Wave on the Ocean

In the same way that a wave settles down into the vast ocean, our thoughts can settle down into the huge expanse of our silent being. Regularly experiencing that calm expanse through meditation broadens our perspective in life, allowing us to act in a calmer and more effective way.

Fortunately, we don't have to go away in solitude to experience silence, nor do we need to be an introverted, silent person to be talented. Research shows that creativity and success in life increases in those who practice Transcendental Meditation.[13]

Enjoy winter's silence along with the serenity within you and get ready to burst forth every day like the dynamism of spring's awakening!

Twenty-Four Hours of Happiness

Occasionally a great new song comes around that captivates me. Pharrell William's song "Happy" is one of those. It is infectious and immediately makes you feel happy. In 2013 it took the world by storm. The song already has over 180 million views on YouTube and a dedicated website 24hoursofhappiness.com, co-branded with the United Nations Foundation. Many countries and cities are making their own music video versions to Pharrell William's song. This wonderful song is truly spreading happiness around the world[14] and is an example of the power of music to uplift and unify different cultures.

There is a field within everyone that is singing with bliss; paradoxically, it is our own silence. By contacting this field through meditation, one spontaneously develops a state of happiness that is independent of the outer ups-and-downs of life. Maharishi said that enlightenment means enjoying twenty-four hours of bliss no matter what is going on in your outer life.

Bhutan is the first country to have a Gross National Happiness[15] index to assess the well-being of its citizens, along with other usual measures such as GDP and PCI for economic growth and prosperity. Hopefully more countries will follow suit. It would be great if growth of happiness were measured in each country, as well as for the world as a whole.

It is heartwarming to know that happiness is growing from the inside out through many people practicing meditation, and that happiness is spreading around the world through this upbeat joyous song, "Happy"!

Happiness Runs in a Circular Motion

Happiness runs in a circular motion
Thought is like a little boat upon the sea
Everybody is a part of everything anyway
You can have everything if you let yourself be.

—Donovan

These profound lyrics have been guiding me my whole life, particularly the last line—"you can have everything if you let yourself be." This line reminds me of a verse from the Bible (Matthew 6:33) that says: "Seek ye first the kingdom of Heaven, and his righteousness; and all these other things shall be added unto you."

My interpretation of these two quotes is that within oneself is a place of heaven—happiness—and if we have that deep real happiness within us, then we truly have everything, for we carry happiness and the fruit of all our desires, the sense of fulfillment, within us wherever we go.

Can We Have Happiness Within?

Donovan answers this question when he says, "if you let yourself be." This phrase "Let yourself be" means to transcend and experience your own silent level of consciousness, which is a state of happiness.

This field of happiness exists within every one of us. It is our own essential nature. We just need to dive into this field of happiness, move in the bliss, and then bring it out into every aspect of the surface values of our life. As Donovan says, "happiness runs in a circular motion." The circular motion is bliss moving within itself, always referring back to itself, self-perpetuating, stirring itself to rise into further waves of happiness.

Object-Referral and Self-Referral

In everyday life we constantly relate to and identify with everything on the outside—our family and friends, our studies, and our work. Referring to objects, or situations on the outside, is called "object-referral." If our happiness is based on our being object-referral, depending upon things "out there," then our happiness can never be lasting because the outside is always changing.

Self-referral is when we refer to, and identify with, that pure state of Being within that is experienced when we transcend. In the state of Self-referral bliss, our happiness is not dependent upon anything on the outside. When we transcend, such as through the Transcendental Meditation (TM) technique, our inner happiness grows stronger every day. We enjoy everything on the outside even more, yet at the same time, we become less dependent on outer changing events for our happiness. Practicing TM is like watering the root of the tree. By doing so, by nourishing the roots, the sap flows to all the different parts—it rises to nourish every branch, leaf, and flower.

Circles of Happiness

Another interpretation of the phrases "happiness runs in a circular motion" and "everything is a part of everything anyway" is that a ripple starts at a point and then spreads out into bigger and bigger circles. We are like the first small point of expanding circles. If we are happy inside then that happiness spreads out around us into bigger and bigger circles of joy. Because we are all connected, we touch everything in the universe with our happiness. If we laugh or smile, the whole universe smiles with us. Fortunately, happiness is contagious; everyone is seeking happiness!

Donovan was inspired to write his song "Happiness Runs in a Circular Motion" after he learned Transcendental Meditation and studied with Maharishi in India. The catchy, sweet melody of the song is definitely happiness-creating!

SECTION 6

SPIRITUAL REFLECTIONS

Self-Empowerment

Today I choose to live by choice, not by chance.
To make changes, not excuses.
To be motivated, not manipulated.
To be useful, not used.
To excel, not compete.
I choose self-esteem, not pity.
I choose to listen to the inner voice, not the random opinion of others.

—Author Unknown

I saw this quote on Facebook. I love how it defines the concept of Self-Empowerment. It states that we should take charge of our life, not letting circumstances or other people control or define us.

Let's break down the word Self-Empowerment. The first word is "Self." There are two aspects to our Self—one is our small self, composed of our surface thoughts, desires, and unique individuality. Then there is the BIG SELF—the deepest aspect of who we are, the silent universal level of our existence. This big "S" Self is our infinite, unbounded, blissful, peaceful nature—our source and essence. The small self is like individual waves on the ocean that are tossed about by the winds that sweep its surface. The big Self is like the vast calm depths of the sea, unmoved by wind or storm.

Meaning of Power

The next word in the term Self-Empowerment is "**empower**." Power means the capacity to exercise control or authority and the ability to accomplish or guide.

Where is the deepest level of power? It is at the source of the power. The light is more powerful the closer we get to the bulb. The more we experience the source of our own power—the big Self—the more power we have to be in control of our lives.

How do we become familiar with our big Self? We can dive into our big Self—our own power—by going beyond the surface level of the mind until we transcend the finest level of the thinking process and experience the pure silence of our Being.

Big Self—Fourth Major State of Consciousness

Research shows that profound physiological changes take place while we meditate, so much so that physiologists have concluded transcending is a fourth major state of consciousness—characterized by a unique combination of restful alertness.[1] In this unique physiological state, the mind is completely calm and still, yet extremely alert. Over time, this inner coherence and order spills into daily activity.

People who meditate often remark that they have become more in control of their lives and are less tossed about by outer circumstances. Even people from stress-ridden populations notice that at first when they learn TM they are less reactive,[2] and then in time they start to find that situations and circumstances are supporting them rather than holding them back. This is true Self-empowerment—empowered intrinsically, from the depths of our being.

One's Essential Nature

There are many valuable organizations today working to help people. I am particularly interested in educational organizations that help young girls become self-empowered.[3] However, to truly empower anyone anywhere, we must give them the experience of their deepest Self—their own essential nature. Once anchored to their inner Self, they gain much more inner fortitude and the motivation to excel in whatever area suits them personally.

The third part of the term Self-empowerment is "ment." Everyone is "meant" to be in the power of their Self and be able to enjoy life to its maximum because the Self is a state of all-powerful love, truth, and bliss. By empowering ourselves with our Self, we can effectively deal with any and all challenging situations—think of Anwar Sadat in solitary confinement! And when we know our Self, we gain the ability to uplift and help our loved ones.

Let's all "choose to be me" and become truly Self-empowered! It is certainly easier.

Unconditioning: Beyond Labels

Growing up in the United States, I was taught that "you can't judge a book by its cover." In truth, this is easier said than done. We are a world of people who, even subconsciously, judge and label others by their gender, speech, skin color, socioeconomic background, sexual orientation, word-on-the-street fame or infamy, and so on. Some of these categories are so ridiculous—and yet they are not easy to escape!

I don't consider myself to be especially judgmental. I've lived all over the world, including in Europe, the Philippines, India, South America, Canada, and Australia, and have friends from many different cultural and socioeconomic backgrounds. However, I still occasionally notice myself labeling, or judging people. It's then that I make a point to start talking to them. Lo and behold, they inevitably prove to be unlike the stereotype I had pegged them for.

I'm thankful every time this happens, because it means that I've received yet one more affirmation to refrain from judging a book by its cover. It also means that, inside me, another judgmental wall—based on mere habit and built from societal conditioning—has been toppled.

We Are Labeled

We may not realize that our persona is created through our upbringing and friends. As a teenager, I was raised to dress a certain way. I'm sure I was labeled "preppy," because I always wore Jack Rogers sandals, cable-knit sweaters and Lily Pulitzer dresses. When I was around seventeen years old, I disengaged myself from that persona and altered my appearance by wearing old blue jeans and long skirts. Anyone looking at me would have labeled me a hippie. The truth is, I was labeling myself—creating a new image based on the trends around me.

Beyond Conditioning

When I learned Transcendental Meditation at the age of 18, I experienced a place of silence within me that was beyond conditioning. It was just me, my truest self, stripped of external images and trappings. Outside of meditation in my daily activities, I started to feel at home with who I really was. I became less swayed by what other people thought of me, and this growing independence brought me a feeling of inner freedom.

Although on occasion I still find myself judging people according to stereotypes, I see more and more beyond superficial values and enjoy discovering who they are inside. We limit ourselves—and the richness that can come from our interactions—when we brand others. Everyone has a gold mine inside, and it's a real joy to discover that treasure. Most people are good. Of course, there are bad apples in the world. They often have had difficulties in their life that caused stress to cover up the goodness deep inside them. Those who have a way to reduce or eliminate stress, for example through a mental technique like TM, have an advantage in dealing with challenging situations.

Oprah Winfrey recently interviewed a man named Shaka Senghor.[4] Mr. Senghor had spent 19 years in prison for second-degree murder. After finishing his sentence, he was still labeled as a criminal, even though he had served his time.

Anyone who has been released from prison is cast for life as potentially dangerous, no matter how much they may have changed. Fortunately, Shaka Senghor is a talented author as well as a criminal justice activist. He has been able to remold his life, against all odds, in an extremely positive way.

At the end of Oprah's interview, there was a short SuperSoul video of a song by Prince Ea (Richard Williams).[5] The lyrics challenge labels and stereotypes attached to the color of our skin and envision a world where people are seen for who they truly are.

Unconditioning Our Mind

Multiple layers of cultural and regional conditioning have been structured in all of us since birth. How can we possibly remove them? The first and most significant step is to "un-condition" our mind by experiencing a state that is beyond conditioning. This is the silent, transcendental level of our consciousness.

As mentioned throughout this book, the technique I have personally found to be most direct to experience transcendence is Transcendental Meditation. To meditate means to think; to transcend means to go beyond the thinking level of our mind and experience pure silence, pure existence, pure Being. The more we experience this unconditional state of Being, the more our lifelong conditioning simply melts away.

In the United States, with the current hyper-charged political climate in which everyone fears terrorists, Afro-Americans fear police, and Mexicans fear being unjustly deported, it is crucial to take a closer look at the mistakes and cruelties stereotyping can cause.

The beauty of our world lies in its mosaic of differences—its diverse cultures and backgrounds. Once we discover within ourselves the common ground of unity among all diversity and start to live it in our daily lives, we will have come a long way towards realizing the ultimate truth of humanity. We can go far beyond the concepts that bind and limit us to see who we truly are.

What I Know to Be True

I recently listened to the audio version of Oprah's book *What I Know For Sure*. In her lively and engaging narration she describes her personal evolution and the spiritual lessons she has learned along the way.

Naturally, after listening to the book, I started to think about "what I know for sure." I keep journals on all my bedside tables wherever I go. When I pulled out my journal to start writing my thoughts on this topic I noticed a poem I had written a short while before. The title of the poem was "What I Know to Be True." Was this a cosmic synchronicity or just a rare coincidence that I had already written a poem exactly on this topic before listening to Oprah's book? The essence of what I know to be the deepest level of truth is the silence that exists within, which I express in the following poem.

What I Know to Be True

What I know to be true—
life is everchanging
like the different waves that dance upon the vast ocean.
What I know to be true is that the eternal now is
our purest Self—
our silence in blissful motion.
What I know to be true
is that the silence behind my thoughts is like the calm blue sky
behind clouds' playful illusions.
What I know to be true is that silence is truth—
the wisdom of the divine
that dissipates all confusion.

The Deeper Meaning of Aloha

As the helicopter lifted off, I felt a thrill of excitement. I was literally inside a small bubble, which lifted into the air and whisked me across the mountains of Kauai, Hawaii. It was breathtaking to fly into the lush valleys and see the many waterfalls—sometimes with rainbows. At times the pilot would fly up the side of a mountain, and when at the peak a sudden vast expanse opened up with magnificent ocean views in the distance.

In an hour, we flew over two-thirds of the island, darting in and out of the valleys, crevices, canyons and flying over the ocean. It was a wonderful way to get an overview of the whole island.

After the helicopter ride, I enjoyed my first swim at Anini beach. On this particular day the glassy, still ocean was a clear turquoise color where I could see down to the bottom. It was another heavenly moment, as well as the prettiest spot I have seen since coming to Kauai.

I have been here almost three weeks and could easily stay longer, but it is time to leave. I have enjoyed every second. The day after I arrived someone said to me, "Are you captured by the magic of Hawaii?" I wondered what she meant, and it is something I have been thinking about the entire time I have been here. I have felt something that I know is deeper than the sweeping views, the lush vegetation and tropical flowers, the delicious mouth-watering fruits, and the kindness of the people. It is the spirit of Aloha.[6]

Aloha is the traditional greeting for hello and goodbye. However, I have learned that there is a deeper meaning. The lesson of Aloha taught to children is:

Aloha is being a part of all, and all being a part of me. When there is pain—it is my pain. When there is joy—it is also mine. I respect all that is a part of the Creator and part of me. I will not willfully harm anyone or anything. When food is needed I will take only my need and explain why it is being taken. The earth, the sky, the sea are mine to care for, to cherish and to protect. This is Hawaiian—this is Aloha![7]

Aloha is also the joyful sharing of life energy. The life energy is the Universal Power, called Mana. Using this power in a loving way is the secret to attaining health, prosperity, and happiness.

It is this deeper spirit of Aloha that has touched me the most during my visit. You feel it in the land, the people, and even in the air. There is an uplifting spiritual energy that has been seeping into my soul. Now that I am leaving, I feel the greatest blessing of being here is gaining the understanding and experience of Aloha. The magic of the island has captured me.

Aloha, aloha, aloha.

Listen to Your Inner Voice

"If only I had listened to my feeling" is a thought we have all probably had at some point in our lives. Other words for this inner voice are "natural instincts," or what some people call "a gut feeling." Top business leaders often say that the reason they are successful is that they were able to go by their gut feelings.

Oprah Winfrey is an example of a successful leader who listens to her inner voice:

> Learning to trust your instincts, using your intuitive sense of what's best for you, is paramount for any lasting success. I've trusted the still, small voice of intuition my entire life. And the only time I've made mistakes is when I didn't listen.[8]

Why Is This Inner Feeling Powerful?

We take most of our information in through the senses—sight, hearing, touch, taste and smell. Our senses connect our outer world with our inner world. Subtler than the senses is our intellect, which discriminates among the experiences coming in from the outer world. However, there is a quiet voice within every one of us that is even deeper than the intellect—our tender feeling level. This level of our being is so delicate and yet so much more powerful than the other levels which are closer to the surface of our existence—such as our senses and our behavior. The feeling level is the closest level to the field of pure silence—Being—pure consciousness.

Access the Unified Field

Maharishi Mahesh Yogi describes the field of pure consciousness as directly mirroring the unified field of natural law identified in quantum physics. Physics tells us that at this ultimate level, all the laws of nature are unified. This is the unified basis that conducts the entire universe in an evolutionary, orderly way at all times.

When our awareness is aligned with the transcendental level of our Being through meditation, then our thoughts and actions are spontaneously more evolutionary, in accord with natural law. This explains why meditators often report they are becoming more attuned to and "in harmony with" their surroundings. They have tapped their inner Self and the power of intuition that exists at the finest level of feeling within.

When we experience silence within, we are more able to hear those quiet whispers that guide us every day. These quiet impulses are also the whispers of creativity that artists and songwriters talk about. The ideas that one catches at this fine feeling level, emerging from pure consciousness, are what filmmaker David Lynch calls the big fish—the great ideas.[9] Lynch refers to the thoughts that we have swimming at the surface of our minds as the little fish. These little thoughts are often born of stress and anxiety. If we are guided by these surface thoughts we may say things we don't mean and do things we later regret.

Some people naturally have greater access to their inner level of feeling or are just stronger in listening and acting according to their intuition. We need to teach all our children to listen to their inner voice and also to act accordingly. They need to understand that a strong person is one who can go by that inner voice that tells them what is right rather than follow what their friends are doing.

The deep rest gained during Transcendental Meditation allows stresses to be released. Our mind becomes clearer and then we are more attuned to those tender feelings deep inside.

As Oprah said:

How many times have you gone against your gut, only to find yourself at odds with the natural flow of things? We all get caught up in the business of doing, and sometimes lose our place in the flow. But the more we can tune in to our intuition, the better off we are. I believe it's how God speaks to us.[10]

I've tried to capture Oprah's sentiment in the following poem:

God's Voice in You

Listen to your innermost feelings
hear the whisper of God in you—
forever divinely appealing,
His thoughts tenderly rising through you.

Listen to your inner voice,
steering your every direction;
fleeting notions and wavering choices cease
in silent wisdom's perfection.

In your heart He forever dwells,
always there to support each need,
gracefully concealed in the bottomless well,
rising to guide every deed.

Act upon God's voice in you;
harmoniously flow in His song.
Every thought, word, and act will sing true,
empowering you in right, weakening all wrong.

Always go by your inner feelings;
hold on tightly to God's leading hand.
Gain trust in His quiet revealings
and walk in the light of His Divine Plan.

My Imagined Commencement Speech

The school year has recently ended, and now is the time when prestigious speakers appear on college campuses to give the traditional commencement speech. This time of year always makes me wonder what I would say if I were asked to give the commencement address at a college or university.

Could I be as inspirational as Oprah[11] or as funny as Jim Carrey?[12] How could I offer insightful commentary like Arianna Huffington, Denzel Washington, Tom Brokaw, and many others? Could I inspire the graduates to know that they truly are the rising leaders of our world? What would I say to let them know that our future is in their hands? How could I paint a picture to portray that they must think big and be the change that they want to see in the world?

These are the questions that run through my mind . . .

The conclusion of many of these speeches is that time spent with family and friends, time spent on the less-beaten path and/or devoted to what you truly wish to do, is more important than the money you accumulate or the deals you may strike in your lifetime.

After thinking my speech out mentally I always come to the same conclusion—I have nothing original to say. So, why not just speak about "nothing"? No one has spoken about "nothing" except maybe Jerry Seinfeld, whose hit show about "nothing" was a tremendous success. I am not saying that I would not do the speech . . . because I would. I actually find "nothing" to be a very powerful topic.

What would I say about "nothing," you ask?

I would start my speech with the usual introductions: "Mr. President, Board of Trustees, faculty, proud parents, and most of all, the graduating class of 2015. Today I am going to talk to you about . . . nothing!"

I would go on to say:

In nothing exists the secret of the universe. In nothing is the secret of everything—an empty, yet percolating field of imagination and creativity. Nothing is the blank paper from where all poems and stories emerge. Nothing is the basis of the empty canvas—where form and color take shape. Nothing is the silence where a symphony of sound emerges to fill our hearts and minds.

It is from within the nothingness of the hollow seed that flowers, trees, fruits, and vegetables spring forth. From nothing all of our creativity rises to write meaningful poems, paint beautiful paintings, and compose harmonious melodies.

If nothing is the basis of all that lives and grows, then nothing is a field of infinite creativity and possibilities. During the past decade progress in theoretical physics describes this concept in a unified-field theory based on the superstring. Even cutting-edge research in the field of neuroscience has revealed what is called a "unified field of consciousness."[13]

This unified field of consciousness, or nothingness, is that one place that unites us all—where we are all equal, coherent, and at peace. This field is a unifying force—the force of love. Being nothing, or empty, it is like the wind, unseen yet moving all things; it is everywhere. Tapping into this unifying force is tapping into our essence of pure unbounded love.

At every moment, this field of nothingness is available to us and creates from within itself the play and display of the entire universe. If we can access the level of lively nothingness, we will imbibe all possibilities and tap into the source of infinite creative intelligence. So, am I saying that nothing is actually a field of infinite intelligence? Yes, precisely!

Everyone has this field of nothingness inside. Inside each one of us exists a field of purity, peace and silence; this is the simplest level of our own Being. We can directly experience this field by taking the time, twenty minutes twice a day, to naturally dive within ourselves through the practice of meditation. I practice Transcendental Meditation, which I find is an effortless means to help me transcend surface thoughts and emotions. With TM, I access the depths of serenity and creativity.

Maharishi Mahesh Yogi used to say, "Do less and accomplish more, do nothing and accomplish everything." My understanding of what he meant by this statement is that when we tend to the deepest level of our Being, everything else comes to fruition more naturally, more effortlessly.

My wish today is that you all directly experience the power of which I am speaking within yourselves. Maybe one day I will hear your commencement speech expressing a personal version of this sentiment to the youth of your time.

May you experience the profundity of nothing, and gain absolutely everything!

Do You Believe in God?

"Do you believe in God?" is a question I am sometimes asked. My first response is to seek clarification by asking, "What do you mean by God?" On an episode of Super Soul Sunday, Oprah Winfrey asked each of her eight guests their definition of God.[14] Everyone had a different answer.

All religions say that God is Love, God is omnipotent, God is omnipresent. Someone once gave me a card with the following quote, "As the self of all, the Lord is loved by all, and with a love with which each person loves his own self."

For me, God is not some-one or some-thing outside of myself based on a belief. God is a tangible, transcendental experience of unbounded love within: a love that is so full it borders on ecstasy; a love so complete that it is not dependent on anything from the outside for its fulfillment; an overflowing love spilling out through my senses, so that everything I see is bathed in the transparent brilliance of love.

I wish I could say that this transcendental love is an everyday experience. What I can say is that it is a growing experience through my regular practice of Transcendental Meditation and its advanced program, the Transcendental Meditation Sidhi Program[SM].

Many people who practice TM report experiences of purest love when they transcend. In the beginning, it is a pleasant feeling of joy. With regular practice, this experience of transcendental joy grows into an experience of pure bliss and love. In time, the feelings of bliss and love start to become ever-present and can be experienced even while engaged in any activity.

The following poem is my best definition and experience of God. I am grateful that this transcendental reality is growing more each day in my life.

He Is My Lord

He who laughs in the form of flowers,
He who smiles in the twinkling of the stars,
He whose song is in the rustling wind,
Whose eternity is in every hour;

He whose whole is in every grain of sand,
He whose heart flows as rushing streams,
He whose radiance is the cool full moon,
Whose love is the essence of man;

He whose warmth is in the dawning morn,
He whose softness is misty raindrops,
He whose light is the rays of the sun,
Whose infinity is every moment born;

He whose greatness is the vast universe,
He whose gentleness is in the falling snow,
He whose joy is the singing birds,
Whose grace is Heaven on Earth;

He whose silence is the depth of the ocean
He whose peace is in the clear blue sky,
He whose bliss is in bubbling brooks,
He is my Lord, my Self, my Silence in motion.

Heaven—Now or Later?

Christians believe that if you have accepted Christ as your savior and have led a good life, you will go to heaven when you die. Hindus believe in reincarnation, which means you must keep coming back to this world until you have achieved the state of enlightenment—*nirvana*—heaven within. The Muslim religion states that if you live a righteous life and believe in God, you will go to paradise when you die.

Is There Proof of Heaven When We Die?

The reality is that there is no proof of what happens after we die. In his book *Proof of Heaven*, Dr. Eben Alexander describes his experience of getting meningitis and going into a coma that defined him as "clinically dead." Fortunately, he miraculously recovered a week later and eventually recounted his experiences and claims he went to heaven. It is an uplifting and hopeful story that heaven exists once we die. There are many stories of people who have had near-death experiences; many claim that they also went to heaven. However, we still can't say for sure that heaven awaits us after death, as there is no concrete scientific proof, only anecdotal evidence. Perhaps heaven is ultimately a subjective experience—heaven is a state of mind.

Where Is Heaven?

Someone once asked Christ when the kingdom of God would come, and he answered: "Neither shall they say, Lo here! or, lo there! for, behold, the kingdom of God is within you." (Luke 17:21)

All religions say that heaven is within. Maharishi stated:

The message of bliss has been the message of all the great Masters of all religions of all times. Christ said, 'The Kingdom of Heaven is within you.' Buddha gave the message of *nirvana*. The Upanishads speak of the same *sat chit ānanda*, eternal bliss consciousness, that is your own Self.[15]

The philosopher and author C.S. Lewis wrote: "Heaven is reality itself; all that is fully real is heavenly."[16]

Live Heaven Now!

If this is true, why not live the reality of heaven now rather than hoping for it when we die? It is rare to meet someone who has as their goal in life "heaven within," even though Christ advised us to "Seek ye first the kingdom of God and His righteousness and all these things shall be added unto you." (Matthew 6:33)

Most people have goals based primarily on material values—they want new cars, a big house, they aspire to fame, to be great musicians or athletes, to make millions of dollars, raise a family, etc. Very few people have heaven as their goal. I think this is because most people don't think that heaven within them is even a possibility.

The possibility of "heaven within" was certainly never discussed in my family as I grew up. It was never mentioned as a possibility by any preacher I heard. At church most services do not offer quiet time to "Be still and know that I am God" (Psalm 46)—the experience of "heaven within." Every time I go to church, I have a desire to close my eyes and start to meditate. Just as I am settling down to a place of peace, it is time to kneel, stand up, or start singing! I admit, singing is enjoyable and certainly can lift one's spirit, but it is not the same as experiencing the steady state of a heavenly peace within.

The New Testament records that Jesus said "heaven is within you," but most people don't know how to experience this profound inner state of joy. Great thinkers, writers, poets, and theologians like Plato, Aristotle, and Ralph Waldo Emerson have written about the experience of this inner state of life. Plato referred to it as "The Good and the Beautiful," Ralph Waldo Emerson as the "Over-Soul." Universal experiences of heaven within have been described throughout time among people from all backgrounds. Clearly it is possible to enjoy this exalted state, even if just for a few moments.

Maharishi has said that heaven within—the state of enlightenment—is our birthright and the very purpose of our existence.

How to Experience Heaven Now

Everyone has heaven within them in the pure silence of their Being, which can be easily and effortlessly accessed through meditation. Heaven within is not a mood or a mere intellectual construct. Heaven within results from physiological and biochemical changes that take place in the mind and body as a result of the regular experience of transcendental consciousness.

Transcendental consciousness, as has been discussed earlier, is a fourth major state of consciousness characterized by a unique state of restful alertness. The mind is awake while the body is in a state of metabolic restfulness deeper even than deep sleep. Scientific studies conducted on TM[17] show improvements on all levels of mind, body, and behavior—life more in the direction of heaven and bliss.

Experiences differ when people first learn Transcendental Meditation. Many experience a quiet pleasantness, while others experience a more all-encompassing state of bliss. In every case, whether delicate or momentous, the direction is clear. Silence grows with regular practice, eventually spilling into activity. There are millions of people around the world who have been meditating for years and are enjoying true inner peace—heaven within, even while engaged in daily life.

Following are two experiences of heaven within from practitioners of Transcendental Meditation, highlighted in my first book *The Transcendental Meditation Technique and the Journey of Enlightenment*:[18]

> As soon as I close my eyes and start TM, there is an all-pervading softness and peace. Thoughts subside as the waves of the ocean settle and become still. I am left in bliss-filled silence. What thoughts may come do not break the surface of the ocean; I remain in a heavenly state of complete stillness and bliss. When I open the eyes after meditation the world is new, I remain an ocean of bliss and

light and silence as I move through my dynamic day. I am so sublimely peaceful and blissful while walking the paths of my life on earth, which themselves merge into that unbounded silence.—USA

Sometimes during meditation golden light pours into my head, as if squeezed through a cloth, filling my head with light. At times, I feel like a newborn baby entering a new dimension of reality made of infinite tenderness, purity, love, and divine wholeness, a heavenly domain.—England

If one could live heaven now, then there would be a greater chance of enjoying it after one dies. Why wait to die to find out if heaven exists? Enjoy heaven here and now!

From Darkness to Light

From the title, you probably think this article is about me overcoming some tragedy like a terrible accident or trauma—that I once was in a dark place, and now I am happy, and the sun is shining. You are half right. However, I am not talking about any outer experience of life that I have overcome. Rather, I am reflecting on the inner journey of the development of consciousness.

What Is Consciousness?

Consciousness is simply awareness, wakefulness, attention. When we observe anything in the outer world we are awake, conscious beings. There are degrees of wakefulness or consciousness. For example, in daily life when we are tired from lack of sleep or overexertion, our mind is not as alert. When we have had a good night's sleep, we wake up the next day feeling fresh and are more awake to the possibilities in the world around us. We have increased awareness.

Another example is the natural expansion of one's territory as one progresses from a baby's consciousness to that of an adult. Early on, an infant has only a very limited view of what constitutes the world: mother, milk, a few family members and toys. As the child grows older his awareness expands to encompass much more of the world; he becomes aware of the whole house, the yard, the surrounding neighbors and neighborhood, then school, and teachers. As development of consciousness continues, a far bigger horizon of the world awaits him.

There is another domain of consciousness to be considered, one that is unchanging and unbounded by space and time. It does not "develop" for it has no place to go; it already is omnipresent and omnipotent. It is the eternal field of pure silence, pure consciousness, pure existence, Being. Through meditation, we become awake to this field of pure eternal consciousness. What are we aware of exactly? We gradually become conscious of our inner silence, which, as we continue regular meditation, turns out to be a vast ocean of silence, of transcendental existence, the basis of ourselves and of everything.

Consciousness Is Made of Light

With continued regular alternation of meditation (the type scientifically shown to be most effective in reducing stress is Transcendental Meditation) and normal daily activity, the awareness of this field of silence opens up to expose that it is more than a flat, dark field of nothingness. Pure consciousness is teeming with energy and intelligence. It is full wakefulness! As stresses dissolve in our physiology, we become more awake, and we start to notice that the inner domain of pure consciousness sparkles with light.

It is similar to walking into a big dark cave. In the beginning, we can only see the darkness. After a few minutes when our eyes have become accustomed to the dark, we begin to see within the darkness the details of the cave.

To sit in meditation bathing in this refined perception of inner light is a deeply fulfilling spiritual experience. It amazes me to think that this light is waiting to shine within every one of the 7.5 billion people on this planet. We reflect outside to the world around us what we experience inside us. We can all become reflectors of this beautiful inner light of consciousness.

Become a Lighthouse

There are so many ways to help the world through charities, social services, business, education, art, music, and so on. If we want the darkness of the clouds covering our precious world to dissipate, it would also help tremendously if more and more people could become lighthouses—dispelling the darkness of war and injustice prevalent in the world today by radiating the inner light of their consciousness.

Ocean of Consciousness

I was extremely fortunate to grow up right on the ocean. Going down to the beach was always a refuge for me. The gentle lapping of the waves soothed and settled me. Looking out over the ocean helped put my problems into perspective, as they would suddenly seem insignificant compared to the infinite expansion of the ocean stretching out to the sky.

Maharishi often spoke about the ocean as an analogy for the mind. He compared the waves on the ocean to our thoughts, and the depths of the ocean to the silent transcendental level of our mind. The process of transcending is like a wave settling into the vastness of the sea.

Maharishi would refer to consciousness in its settled state as one unbounded ocean of consciousness in motion. The most settled state of our mind—pure consciousness—is not a flat, empty silence, but a dynamic field—always flowing within itself. It is teeming with energy and intelligence.

If you go to Florida for vacation to escape the gray, cold winter, as you dive into the ocean remember you can also dive into the ocean of your own consciousness and come out refreshed and rejuvenated. Actually you don't have to go to Florida—you can dive into your Self twice a day wherever you are, any time of the year.

SECTION 7

MEDITATION

Meditation Versus Transcending

People come up to me all the time and say things like, "when I walk or go jogging, or when I am sitting on the beach looking out over the ocean, that is my meditation." Just recently, I was in a shop owned by a woman who makes hand-painted pillows. She said to me, "Painting on pillows is my meditation." Naturally, people often say that praying is their form of meditation. Praying, walking, golfing, being in nature, sitting on the beach, etc., all provide a quiet time for reflection. After all, to "meditate" (*dharana*) literally means to "think."

We all need time for quiet reflection, whether we work, stay at home with children, or go to school. Quiet reflection helps anyone gain perspective on life's multitude of situations. It involves thinking and occurs during the waking state of consciousness.

The Difference between Meditating and Transcending

There is a big difference, however, between reflecting quietly, enjoying the beauty of nature, praying, and the experience of transcending. "Transcending" means to "go beyond." When we practice TM, we go beyond the surface level of our thinking process where all thoughts, even quiet reflection, take place. We transcend thought entirely and arrive at a state of no thought—the field of pure consciousness, Being.

Transcendence—a Major Fourth State of Consciousness

In other words, we transcend the waking state of consciousness and shift into the fourth major state of consciousness, characterized by restful alertness. A comparison of 31 previously conducted studies[1] showed that the experience of transcendental consciousness, as experienced during the practice of the Transcendental Meditation technique, produced a level of physical rest deeper than eyes-closed resting, and nearly twice as deep as deep sleep. One parameter of this state of deep rest is reduced basal skin conductance. Other indicators are a marked decrease in respiratory rate and in plasma lactate. Plasma lactate is a chemical byproduct of stress.

An important point to note is that these physiological changes occur spontaneously as the mind effortlessly settles to transcendental consciousness—a state of inner peace.

This fourth major state, while extremely restful, is unlike sleep. When sleeping, the mind loses awareness altogether. During transcendental consciousness, the body rests deeply and at the same time the mind is alert. The brain wave patterns differ markedly between waking, dreaming, and sleeping states as indicated by alpha-1 brain wave coherence.[2] Thus, transcendental consciousness is termed by researchers to be a state of *restful alertness*.

People who practice Transcendental Meditation, as compared to other types of meditation and contemplation, report that their experiences of walking in nature, painting, playing music, being in church—their times for quiet reflection—are richer. They also notice that they are more awake to the beauty around them at each moment.

Adding the experience of transcendence to one's daily routine through a technique like Transcendental Meditation will enrich all aspects of life. It is like watering the root to enjoy the fruit!

Are All Meditations the Same?

One of the most common questions I am asked is how Transcendental Meditation differs from other forms of meditation. There are many types of meditation, are all of these practices the same?[3]

Very often people will come to me expressing that they have tried to meditate, but find it difficult. They say that they have too many thoughts and can't quiet the mind. Instead of settling down in meditation, they are restless and bored and want to jump out of their seat.

Most Meditation Techniques Are Difficult

Most meditation techniques involve effort: effort to silence the mind, effort to concentrate on one thought or image, and effort to watch the breath. In guided meditation one is told to move from one visualization to the next, thus keeping the mind continuously engaged on the conscious thinking level—the surface of the mind. Trying to stay focused on a thought or an image is difficult for most people. The mind tends to wander and consequently does not settle down to quieter levels.

Trying to Concentrate Is Unnatural

The ocean is a good analogy to explain the different types of meditation. On the surface of the ocean, we have waves, sometimes rough, other times calm. These waves are like the surface level of our mind. According to the Laboratory of Neuro Imaging, the average person has approximately 70,000 thoughts per day.[4] Thoughts can be more if we are stressed or less if we are rested and balanced. Either way, we have lots of waves!

The purpose of practicing mindfulness meditation is for the practitioner to be present, dispassionately observing the waves in the mind when engaged in thoughts. Meditation techniques involving concentration aim to keep attention focused on the thought and keep bringing the attention back to that thought. This is difficult and tedious and requires discipline to practice. If what one is trying to concentrate on is not pleasing to the mind, the mind will wander, seeking fulfillment else-where. Concentration techniques may strain the mind to try to focus on something that is not particularly engaging.

Maharishi Mahesh Yogi teaches that the mind will automatically stay concentrated and engaged with something that is enjoyable, without any effort or need for discipline. The TM technique allows the mind to naturally settle down to quieter levels. It works because of the natural tendency of the mind to seek happiness. The quieter, more settled levels of our mind are extremely charming and the mind will automatically be drawn there. The mind effortlessly turns in that direction—inward—when given the opportunity to do so. It automati-cally goes to more subtle levels, with no effort on our part.

Returning to the analogy of the ocean, instead of observing the waves on the surface, or forcing the mind to stick with one particular wave, with TM we transcend the waves and dive deep into the pleasing blissful silence at the depths of the ocean.

Transcendence—the Goal of Meditation

It is a common misconception that to rein in or completely get rid of thoughts is the goal of meditation. Trying to control thoughts during meditation is a wrong understanding, which unfortunately pervades society and makes most people feel like they don't even want to learn to meditate. People feel they are so active that there is no way that they can quiet or empty their mind.

Enlightenment—the Goal of Transcendence

The transcendent is beyond space and time. It is a field of eternal silence, yet also total wakefulness. With regular practice this state becomes estab-lished so that even in activity, one enjoys that inner peace and happiness.

Eventually, the state of transcendence takes over so completely that everything in the outer world is experienced as a wave of the same silence experienced in deep meditation. This inner silence experienced along with dynamic activity is the state of enlightenment. It is as if the deep inner value of life expands to overtake the whole of our outer world. All of life is then experienced as a state of oneness, a state of unity. This is enlightenment—the ultimate goal of all forms of meditation.

Everyone has to choose what meditation technique is most comfortable for them. Personally, I have learned that strain and discomfort are counterproductive. I now tend to favor what is natural, easy, effective, and enjoyable in all aspects of my life.

Tim Ferriss, Dr. Tara Brach, and Some Misconceptions about Transcendental Meditation

I recently listened to a podcast[5] of Timothy Ferriss (author of *The 4-Hour Workweek: Escape 9–5, Live Anywhere, and Join the New Rich*) interviewing Tara Brach, PhD in clinical psychology, renowned author and lecturer on Buddhist thought in the West.

During the interview, Mr. Ferriss mentions that he practices Transcendental Meditation and asks Dr. Brach for her opinion on the practice of TM. Below is Brach's perspective and then my own comments in response.

> TM is primarily a concentrated practice: You are taking a mantra, or a set of sacred words, and repeating them and repeating them and the benefit of concentration, which is the narrowing of the lens of focus, is that it actually collects the attention and the mind gets quiet. And when the mind is quiet, there can be experiences of bliss and serenity and peace and so on. That's what TM does; it gives you a break from that incessant inner dialogue, and the more you practice it, the more easy it is to collect the mind.
>
> . . .

For me the limitation is—it doesn't allow you to see into the nature of reality; and by that I mean—it doesn't bring a kind of presence that allows you to sense what is actually happening now. Most of our understanding of reality is conceptual—we have ideas about things, and to really have a clear penetrating insight, we need to be present. TM aims the mind at something, but it doesn't open the attention so that whatever arises, you start learning how to be with it. To me, the power and freedom of mindfulness is you start getting the knack of being with whatever arises. One of the things I'm very aware of is that most of us are aware of our mortality, and we're tensing against what could go wrong.[6]

There are several elements of Dr. Brach's statements that I would like to address.

First, she says that Transcendental Meditation involves concentration. As I have explained throughout this book, the technique of TM does not involve concentration whatsoever. The state of transcendental consciousness[7] produced by TM is an experience of pure bliss consciousness, and the mind will naturally settle down to its own blissful nature without any concentration or effort, when provided the right conditions. The TM technique provides those conditions.

Let's take an example from everyday life. If you are talking to someone, and your favorite music comes on in the next room, your attention will naturally shift away from the conversation and toward the music. You didn't intellectually decide to shift your focus, and you didn't expend any effort to do it: the attention-shift happened automatically. This is due to the nature of the mind to seek what interests it most. TM is based on this natural tendency of the mind. It doesn't involve the slightest degree of concentration and in fact, if there *were* any concentrative efforts, the practice would not be Transcendental Meditation, because such efforts would obstruct transcending.

Second, Dr. Brach is correct in saying that TM uses a mantra, which leads to a state of bliss and serenity. However, there is one important yet subtle point of distinction—the purpose of the mantra is not to narrow the mind's focus, but rather to experience finer, more expanded states until one experiences the state of transcendence—a state of unbounded awareness. This is almost the exact opposite of "collecting" and quieting the mind. We have already discussed that TM results in a unique fourth state of consciousness—transcendental consciousness—with characteristics corresponding to restful alertness. This result is significantly different from the minor (or complete lack of) physiological changes resulting from concentration practices.

Reality Is as You Are

The next misconception Dr. Brach mentions is that TM is limited because it "doesn't allow you to see into the nature of reality" and "be present to the moment." Maharishi has pointed out that your reality is as you are; the world is as you are. As we have seen, the deepest and most universal reality is transcendental—an unbounded, cosmic field, present within everyone. Alternating Transcendental Meditation with normal activity day after day (this is the TM "program") powerfully cultures the nervous system to maintain broad comprehension of transcendental consciousness along with the sharp focus of daily life. The mind gets in the habit of expansion in both directions: to its infinite value and, at the other extreme, to its point value. In fact, only when we have the experience of transcendental consciousness are we capable of truly "seeing into the nature of reality," as Dr. Brach describes, and living fully and completely "in the moment."

Stages of Growing Enlightenment

The first step of enlightenment is the experience of transcendental consciousness, spontaneous pure "mindfulness," a natural state when the attention goes within. This is the cosmic universal level of the mind, accessed at the source of thought. The experience of transcendental consciousness provides profoundly deep rest, which enables the body to throw off stresses and imbalances. Stresses cloud the mind's naturally settled and focused state, preventing us from being fully present "in the moment." Gradually, the nervous system becomes completely stress-free.

The second step is stabilizing this level of transcendental consciousness in daily activity, which occurs through regular meditation and activity until the nervous system can maintain both unique styles of functioning at the same time. This stage is called cosmic consciousness[8]—when we maintain awareness of the cosmic, non-changing, universal level of life while engaged in our day-to-day activities. This is a state of naturally being mindful and alert at all times, since at this point the nervous system is free of stress and strain.

When we have gained cosmic consciousness, we maintain awareness of the non-changing, universal level of life while engaged in waking, sleeping, and dreaming.

In my view, the basis of true mindfulness is in first experiencing the deepest level of the eternal reality of life. People who have been regularly practicing Transcendental Meditation have progressively clearer experiences of the unbounded level of their mind. In time, this silent, expanded, limitless state is not only experienced more and more during meditation, but also while engaged in dynamic activity. Consequently, TM practitioners naturally become more present in everything they do without any intellectualizing or trying to be present.

Following is an experience of someone who has been practicing TM regularly for several years:

> I have had the experience of feeling, or being, the huge unbounded field of consciousness—that is who I am, and I see the sequence of time in my individual life as if I am viewing it from a distance. I see time (my life) coming from the past and continuing into the future, like a train, and I see where I am now. When I come out of meditation, I see my self as if stepping onto that train of activity. I am watching, my individuality simply steps into activity and goes through the necessary motions that need to be done, but I am separate from it; the activity does not touch my essential nature, my essential Self does not become involved in it.[9]

Unity Consciousness—Going the Whole Way

The well-intentioned Dr. Brach concludes that Transcendental Meditation does not take you "the whole way," i.e., to the state of being mindful; to being with whatever arises—"present to things that come and go in life."

Maharishi would say that the "whole way" is to live Unity Consciousness—an even more refined state than Cosmic Consciousness. In Unity Consciousness we are awake to the entire world as an expression of our universal Self—as waves on the ocean of our unbounded Being. We see the infinite, transcendental value of our Self shining through the boundaries of every object. We still perceive the boundaries, but unity dominates our awareness. Perception is no longer overshadowed—our essential nature shines forth like the sun illuminating all. This is realization of the ultimate reality—enlightenment. Maharishi describes this state in his commentary on the Bhagavad-Gītā:

> The height of realization . . . is to realize the supreme oneness of life in terms of one's own Self. No diversity of life is able to detract from this state of supreme Unity. One who has reached It is the supporter of all and everything, for he is life eternal. He bridges the gulf between the relative and the Absolute . . . Yoga [Union] in this state has reached its perfection; there is no level of Union higher than this that he has gained. He stands established on the ultimate level of consciousness.[10]

Lastly, in the interview Dr. Brach mentions that she sees the gift of meditation as learning how to "be" with living and dying. According to Maharishi's teachings, the best way to learn about living and dying is to directly experience the transcendental level of existence, for it is the very essence of existence—the immortal realm of eternal life underlying all that is born and all that passes away.

Reduction of stress is an important step in normalizing the physiology so that it can function in an integrated and healthy manner, but "busting" stress is, after all, a side benefit of TM. Let's "go the whole way" and enjoy the natural outcome of this technique: growing in unity consciousness. Enlightenment is the very purpose of our birth and we should choose the most effective and direct path.

Can Listening to Music
Help Me Transcend?

I love listening to music! Different music obviously has different effects. I will often let my mood select the type of music to listen to in that moment. Some music makes me want to dance and sing. Other types of music penetrate deep into my heart and uplift my emotions. There is also music that has a settling effect on my mind and body.

When the mind settles down to quieter levels, this is the beginning process of transcending.

What Is Transcending?

By now we understand that the process of transcending takes one inside, from the surface, active level of the thinking mind to more refined, quieter levels of the thinking process.

Going to a loud rock concert would not help one to settle down and would probably stimulate the body to want to dance. Dancing to music is certainly joyful, but this activity will move the mind and body outwards, in the opposite direction of transcending. If you are listening to soothing music with eyes closed, it will most likely have a settling effect on the physiology and may aid in setting the stage for transcending.

Transcending takes us beyond all our thoughts to experience the field of pure silence—the cosmic, unbounded level of our being. Although music can aid us in settling down, to completely transcend we have to go beyond the music.

What Is Transcendence?

Transcendence is when we go beyond even the quietest level of the mind and experience the source of thought, the purest, innermost level of our silent awareness.

Hear the Music of Silence

Music, including the classical music of India known as Gandharva Veda, can help with approaching transcending. However, if you want the fastest possible way to transcend, meditation is the royal path.

On the other hand, it is worth mentioning that being completely present to my own transcendental experience and internal silence has also been a powerful musical experience.

The Scottish writer Thomas Carlyle said, "See deep enough, and you see musically; the heart of nature being everywhere musical, if you can only reach it."[11]

How to Talk about Meditation to a Child

Young children are incredibly inquisitive and also extremely sensitive. When my niece was around four or five years old, she would sometimes sit in my room while I meditated. Occasionally she would camp outside the room on her sleeping bag and wait until I finished meditating. Although she did not understand what meditation was, she sensed that it was something good.

How does one explain meditation to a child? Maharishi often uses the example of a rose. On the outside we see the rose petals, green leaves, and the stem. On the inside, we know there is something unseen—the sap—the one guiding element for the whole flower. This is analogous to ourselves as well. On the outside of our body we are the eyes, nose, hands, feet, etc. Inside the body we have thoughts, feelings and most importantly, consciousness, which is not apparent from the outside, but which is the guiding force for all the activity of the body and behavior.

Maharishi explains[12] that both outer and inner values of life are guided by the inner value, the unseen sap in the flower, the home of all the laws of nature. In meditation we experience the deepest, most silent level of our consciousness, which he equates with the home of all the laws of nature.

These points may seem advanced for a young child, but I have learned that children are smarter than we think. The simplicity and innocence of the Transcendental Meditation practice is similar to the simplicity of a child's nature. TM is so simple to practice that anyone, even a ten year old, will automatically settle down into their own silent Being.

At the age of four, children can learn a walking meditation,[13] with eyes open, and then at age ten they can learn the Transcendental Meditation technique, in which one sits with eyes closed.

SECTION 8

YOGA

In the Vicinity of Coherence (Yoga), Hostile Tendencies Are Eliminated

T at sannidhau vairatyāghaḥ is a verse from the Yoga Sūtra (2.35)[1] that means, "In the vicinity of coherence (Yoga), hostile tendencies are eliminated." We have all heard the sayings, "united we stand, divided we fall" and "strength lies in unity." Even "divide and conquer" is related to this principle; to weaken the enemy, break up their solidarity.

One of the universal principles in nature is that internally coherent systems possess the ability to repel external disruptive influences, while incoherent systems are easily penetrated by disorder from the outside. In physics this principle of nature is called the Meissner Effect, after the physicists who discovered the phenomenon in 1933, Walther Meissner and Robert Ochsenfeld. This principle applies to all levels, from the atomic level of a superconductor all the way to the macro level of human society. When there is some weakness in the coherence of a system, stress or tension builds up around that point and eventually breaks through!

After the tragic events in Newtown, Connecticut on December 14, 2012,[2] the whole U.S. national discussion focused on gun control and reducing children's exposure to violence in movies and video games. While this discussion is important to have, we need a multilayered approach to solve the outbreak of violence—an approach that includes reducing stress and creating more coherence. Chronic insecurity, anxiety, fear, frustration, polarization, and anger result in situations that eventually lead to crime, economic instability, and governmental gridlock. The reverse is also true: reduced stress results in positive emotions and societal coherence, as indicated by positive trends such as increased U.S. patent applications, self-reported improved relationships at work and at home, decreased domestic violence, etc.

These days political leaders are exhibiting high degrees of incoherence; they cannot seem to get together to solve or agree on anything. Maharishi describes that government leaders are, in fact, just an innocent mirror of the collective consciousness of the nation.[3] If we want to have wiser national leadership and fair and just governmental policies, we need to reduce stress and create more coherence in our own lives and in our families, because individuals and families are the basic units of society. Our grassroots coherence will help reduce stress in society as a whole.

Research on those practicing Transcendental Meditation shows an immediate reduction of stress and anxiety, as well as increased coherence in the brain,[4] even right from the first meditation. In electroencephalogram (EEG) studies, TM meditators show synchronicity of the right and left brain hemispheres. This means that right from the start, their brains are becoming more awake and their neurons are firing in synchrony. This demonstrates growth of total brain functioning: all possible mental resources are available for the task at hand. With continued practice, that internal coherence grows, even outside meditation.

Taking the time twenty minutes twice a day to experience the deepest level of our silence within is so important. In addition to dissolving stress in our body and mind and creating more orderly brain functioning, this is the one experience in life that unites us all.

After a tragedy like Newtown or 9/11, America always rallies and comes together, but after some time it is back to divisive politics as usual. Meditating daily is one way that we as individuals can come together on a deeper level to concretely reduce violence and create coherence in society, without depending on government policies. A time of silence every day is also a meaningful way to honor the precious, innocent lives that were lost in Newtown, Connecticut.

Meditating is one way we can become united, thus helping to neutralize the buildup of any negativity before it bursts forth. In unity we can accomplish anything as a nation!

International Yoga Day

On June 21, 2015, International Yoga Day was celebrated worldwide. Maharishi Mahesh Yogi gave the world an understanding of a deeper reality of what yoga (union) is—the unity of life that is available on every level of the body, mind, consciousness, society, extending even to the unity of world peace. This understanding is different from how yoga is commonly understood these days, which is mainly limited to the physical body and physical postures and exercises.

How Yoga Works

Maharishi has brought to light that yoga—perfect harmony—starts from the field of unity (*samādhi*), silent and blissful, deep within each and every one of us. The classic ancient text on Yoga was cognized thousands of years ago by an ancient Vedic seer, Maharishi Patanjali. In his exposition, Patanjali explains that the body of yoga encompasses the entire field of creation, inner and outer. Patanjali's Yoga Sūtra[5] elucidates eight "limbs" of one body: they grow simultaneously and in proportion to one another, just as a baby's bodily limbs grow simultaneously and in conjunction to the whole body. It's not that an arm suddenly springs forth fully grown and then the legs start! Yoga is about the wholeness of life and the growth of wholeness from within, always maintaining the scale and proportion of wholeness in every part.

Modern research on Transcendental Meditation[6] indicates that this is indeed the case. In TM, during experience of transcendental consciousness (Patanjali calls it *samādhi*), mind and body are simultaneously improved, resulting in benefits to every area of life, including:

- reduced stress and anxiety
- reduced heart disease
- reduced diseases of all kinds
- increased energy and efficiency
- improvement in relationships

Yoga in the World Today

The International Day of Yoga[7] calls for an upsurge of the unifying influence in world consciousness to help meet the demands of the time. The need of our time is for *samādhi*—transcendental consciousness, to harmonize and bring balance and stability among nations. On the world stage, large groups experiencing transcendental consciousness have been scientifically shown to reduce crime, accidents, and warfare, and increase peace.[8]

"Only a new seed will yield a new crop." It is time for the seed of unity, Yoga, to be sown in every heart to bring peace into the world.

Maharishi on Yoga

"The advice is to continue yoga on the physical level, and start and continue yoga on the mental level, and start to continue Yoga on the intellectual level, and live in daily life yoga on the Self level. On all levels of life—physical, mental, intellectual, and on the level of Transcendental Being—on all levels, yoga will help you to progress in every way, in every field of life.

"Yoga means Unity. Unity means that we are bringing unified wholeness more and more into the field of diversity. One of the Yoga sayings is that 'Yoga is superior action.' When you want a better quality of action, then you practice Yoga—and Yoga on all levels.

"Transcendental Meditation is all Yoga. I had to call it Transcendental Meditation—a new name—because I felt Yoga has been commonly understood in terms of physical exercises. That is also a Yoga, but it is on a level of its own. Then, there is mental Yoga, intellectual Yoga, and then the Self-Referral Yoga—Self-Referral Consciousness, the Unified field of all the Laws of Nature, the field of Consciousness, Consciousness, which is more basic to all the physical levels.

Yoga is a good word, but it should be properly understood and practiced, and the result will be holistic evolution of life."[9]

Want More than Downward Dog?

In 2013, the Smithsonian Museum featured the art world's first international exhibit on the visual history of yoga, in *Yoga: the Art of Transformation*.[10] Another sign of the growing popularity of yoga is that the Sackler Gallery raised $174,000 through crowdfunding for the exhibit, helped by 600 donors and others looking to enhance their yoga practice.

The many types of yoga offered in the marketplace today are overwhelming. There is Bikram Yoga, Hatha Yoga, Kundalini Yoga, Iyengar Yoga, Anusara Yoga, trauma sensitive yoga, yoga for anger,[11] yoga for improving your posture,[12] Christian yoga, yoga to cure desk ailments,[13] yoga for increasing patience,[14] yoga for back pain,[15] yoga for energy, fizzy yoga,[16] yoga for sleep,[17] yoga for runners,[18] yoga for pain,[19] military yoga, broga yoga for men,[20] laughing yoga,[21] yoga for those over 50,[22] and of course, yoga for toddlers.[23]

All these types of yoga use physical postures (the more authentic term for these postures that Patanjali uses in his Yoga Sūtra is *asana*), and sometimes breathing exercises. The immense popularity of yoga is simply because it is good for you and also feels good—you most likely feel lighter and more flexible, peaceful and calm, after a "yoga" session. However, yoga asanas, while important, are only a small part of the Yoga Sūtra of Patanjali.

Want More than Downward Dog?

Yoga asanas, or physical positions, definitely play a role in aligning mind and body. Focusing on the body, stretching, and the long periods of calm focus all serve to reduce stress and enhance health. If you limit your practice to only physical postures, however, you are missing out on the real essence and original meaning of yoga—the growth of wholeness of life, enlightenment.

The word yoga is derived from the Sanskrit verb, *yog*, which means to yoke, or to join together, indicating unification, or joining, of individual awareness with its source in unbounded universal pure consciousness.

Maharishi Mahesh Yogi describes the state of Yoga in his commentary on the Bhagavad-Gītā as follows:

> The height of realization . . . is to realize the supreme oneness of life in terms of one's own Self. No diversity of life is able to detract from this state of supreme Unity. One who has reached It is the supporter of all and everything, for he is life eternal. He bridges the gulf between the relative and the Absolute . . . Yoga [Union] in this state has reached its perfection; there is no level of Union higher than this that he has gained. He stands established on the ultimate level of consciousness.[24]

The Yoga Sūtra of Patanjali[25] states that *yogash chitta vritti nirodha:* "Yoga is the complete settling of the activity of the mind." When the awareness transcends and experiences the source of thought, the state of yoga—unity or *samādhi*—the mind, intellect, emotions, and body are fully integrated. Meditation single-handedly takes care of integrating, or uniting, all these levels.

Are You Finding Meditation Difficult?

A common misconception about meditation is that it is difficult, requiring concentration or contemplation, both of which can strain the mind and cause headaches and irritability. In contrast, the experience of the state of yoga is effortlessly achieved, for it is the most blissful, completely fulfilling state of life, and if given the right direction, the mind will naturally settle down to quieter levels, eventually transcending even the quietest level and experiencing pure consciousness—the state of yoga.[26]

Yoga and the State of Enlightenment

Many yoga practitioners who add Transcendental Meditation to their daily routine find it provides a deeply satisfying dimension of silence, awareness, and appreciation to their life as a whole; it also enriches their yoga practice. They feel a great leap in their spiritual evolution. This is because the experience of *samādhi*—transcendental consciousness—is the basis and ultimate goal of a truly blissful yoga practice.

Samādhi, literally "even intellect," is the basis and the bridge to enlightenment. Enjoy bending, but to get the maximum benefits of yoga also enjoy transcending!

Yoga and Enlightenment

I have been doing yoga since 1973 and absolutely love it. I come out of yoga class feeling light, relaxed, and definitely stretched out in all directions. These days, the ancient practice of yoga has become so mainstream that it is even being offered at my family's conservative beach and tennis club!

Yoga has been investigated by the scientific world and consistently shows excellent results for increased health and well-being.[27] Most people, however, still think that yoga only consists of physical exercises and stretching.

In ancient India, where yoga originally came from, the word yoga means "union": of mind, intellect, emotions, and body, as well as union of the individual with the universal. Yoga is regarded as a physical, mental, and spiritual discipline. Ultimately the goal of yoga was, and still is, enlightenment. This means one is living in unity consciousness—a state in which one realizes the grand oneness of life, whereby no diversity or stress in life is able to detract from this state of oneness.

The deepest experience of yoga is the complete settling of the mind—the experience of transcendental consciousness—a unique fourth state of consciousness beyond the regular waking, dreaming, and sleeping states, which can be experienced and systematically developed through meditation.

I have been a teacher of Transcendental Meditation since 1973. I use this technique of meditation because it is the most natural and effortless technique that I have found. I want to emphasize the importance of the word effortless in regards to Transcendental Meditation, because many of the people who tell me that they do yoga have also tried other forms of meditation, but find it difficult to be quiet. Instead of relaxing, they are restless and have lots of thoughts.

The settled experience of transcendental consciousness during Transcendental Meditation unites the mind, intellect, emotions, and body. This state is also an experience of union of the individual with the universal.

This experience of unity first grows in meditation and then over time it grows even into one's activity—resulting in the experience of unity consciousness. This is the growing state of enlightenment and the true meaning of the practice of yoga.

The combination of yoga postures and meditation accelerates the growth of enlightenment because yoga strengthens and tones the physiology and also settles the mind and body. It sets the stage for a more profound meditation. Meditation then allows the mind to settle into even deeper levels of calm and inner peace.

The combination of stretching and transcending provides a powerful means for the unfoldment of higher states of consciousness, enlightenment.

SECTION 9

WOMEN

Birds of a Feather Flock Together

Sometimes women love to spend time with women, and men with men, just as sometimes children like to be with children, and teenagers with teenagers. It's natural. Can we as women use that time of getting together with other women to enhance our spiritual lives and to improve the world on a deeper level?

In the United States, women comprise more than half of the workforce, and many are also the main caregivers for their families. Coming home at the end of a workday and attending to children, chores, and meal preparation can be overwhelming and exhausting. Yet we often put others' needs before our own.

Taking time to nourish ourselves is sometimes the best way to nourish our family and to be most efficient in our responsibilities.

A way to nourish ourselves most deeply is through the experience of inner silence, our own pure consciousness. Within everyone, male or female, is an ocean of soothing softness, renewable energy, and release from the stress of the day. The experience of silence is the purest form of being pampered, the highest form of luxury.

When practicing meditation together in a group, especially with other women, the softness of the atmosphere created by the refined physiologies of women is an outer soothing experience that enhances the inner experience of the nourishing ocean of inner silence. This increased feeling of softness creates a richer spiritual experience, and also helps to melt the hardness and aggression so prevalent in the world today.

Women are taking a more active role, yet often a spiritual approach, in trying to solve the many problems we face today. We are all interconnected more than ever via the internet and social media. What's happening in the 24/7 news cycle and social media affects the entire collective consciousness. When we come together to meditate, we transcend the outer turmoil reflected in the collective consciousness, and actually nourish and soften the collective consciousness from the deepest level of Being.

Let's unite as women to deepen our own spirituality, while at the same time radiating a tangible softening effect in the world around us!!

A United State of Women— Another Perspective

A video about the United State of Women[1] recently appeared on my Facebook page. The video featured many famous women, including Michelle Obama, Oprah Winfrey, Meryl Streep, and Tina Fey. When women come together, they are an incredibly powerful force that has the ability to change the world.

It was a group of determined, impoverished, female factory workers in England in the late 1800s who ignited the beginning of the Suffragette movement, which eventually won women the right to vote in England and influenced many other countries to eventually follow suit. In 1999, during the second Liberian civil war, it was a group of Liberian women who went to Ghana and sat outside the government buildings until the warring factions came to a peace agreement. It was women in Iceland who went on strike[2] for a day in 1975, who eventually achieved civil rights for the women of Iceland, and who have since kept their country at the top of the list of many proud achievements in economics, education, judicial and penal systems, and civil liberties.

Now women like Gloria Steinem and Eve Ensler are taking up the charge to stop violence against women around the world. Globally, many admirable women are speaking out to increase fairness and much-needed justice for women.

A United State of Our Minds

Women's issues definitely unite women, bringing them together to find solutions. Is there something deeper that unites women and also men? Is there a field, or a state, of unity itself that naturally unites us all?

Every person on this planet has active and quieter levels of the mind. The active surface level is our thoughts, our to-do lists, our plans. The quieter levels are our feelings and intuitions. The content of these different levels of mind are unique to each person and certainly no two people can have the same thoughts and feelings all at the same time. In this sense, everyone is unique.

But there is a state that exists beyond all thoughts and feelings. It is the state of pure silence that has been discussed extensively in these pages. The unique attribute of silence is that my silence is the same as your silence. Silence is silence no matter who you are or where you live. Every one of the billions of people on this planet has this state of silence within, although every person is a different expression, or container, of it.

The Unified Field of Natural Law

Scientists have documented this state of restful alertness, inner silence, as a major fourth state of consciousness[3] called transcendental consciousness, which is different from the waking, dreaming, and sleep states of consciousness. Maharishi equated this state with the unified field of natural law in quantum physics.[4] Unified field theories locate a single, universal, unified field of intelligence at the basis of all forms and phenomena in the universe. Millions of times more fundamental and more powerful than the nuclear force, the unified field is the ultimate source of the order displayed throughout the vast universe.

It is interesting that research shows the experience of this field of silence creates more orderliness in brain functioning. Neuroscientists have found that during the practice of TM, the brain produces coherent alpha waves.[5] This distinct brain pattern corresponds to the state of silence, or inner wakefulness, expansion, and bliss.

When one transcends, even from the first meditation, the alpha-1 brainwaves become synchronous. This coherence spreads throughout the brain and is strongest in the prefrontal cortex—the seat of your brain's executive judgment.

A coherent brain reflects a state of unity. When we are coherent and harmonious within, that unity will naturally spill out into our surroundings.

As women, we are the creators of life and, as mothers, the main nourishers of our families. Naturally inherent in us is the tendency to be nourishers and uniters of our world family. If women can also meditate together, this nourishing, uniting power will be amplified many times in the environment.

Many published studies[6] show that when one percent of a given population practice Transcendental Meditation in an area, the crime rate goes down and positive trends increase.

All Change Begins Within

In the United State of Women video Oprah said, "We need to turn struggle into strength." Other women made the astute comment that, "When we do better, then everyone does better." Of course, when we are happier the world around us is better.

We need to create change on every level of life, but the most fundamental and powerful change comes from the deepest level. In truth, all change begins within.

As Michelle Obama said in the video, "We stand stronger when we stand together." We will truly stand stronger when we stand united in our silence within.

The Power of Women Gathering: The Goddess is in Connections

History was made Saturday, January 21st, 2017 when more than three million people came together to march in Washington, D.C., cities across the United States, and in countries all around the world. Young, old, black, white, Christians, Muslims, Jews—people from all ethnicities and religions gathered together to protest. Although the march addressed many specific issues facing women, the overall theme was "Women's Rights are Human Rights and Human Rights are Women's Rights."

The feeling of unity, purpose, and love in the air was palpable even to a bystander watching on TV. A few of the more positive signs that I particularly liked were "Love Trumps Hate," "If Mom's Not Happy, Nobody's Happy," "Girls just want to have FUNdamental rights," "No Longer Am I Accepting the Things I Cannot Change, I Am Changing the Things I Cannot Accept."

The Goddess is in Connections

A bigger phenomenon than women just marching on the streets occurred on January 21st. It was the beginning of a revolution united by the single purpose to restore basic human values of goodness. As Michelle Obama said at the Democratic Convention, "When they go low, we go high." Almost three million women marching together rose very high, touching all the corners of the world.

Gloria Steinem captured the feeling of the day when she said, "God maybe is in the details, but the Goddess is in connections!" Women are connectors because they engage each other from heart to heart. Mothers never want to see their children go to war. Women don't want to fight and conquer; instead they would rather hug and talk, and solve problems through communication and discussing each other's ideas.[7]

Women protesting around a united purpose have proven to be an effective means for change during times of great need. However, there is an even more powerful level that can bring profound change.

Change on the Basis of Non-Changing Silence

No two people on this planet are the same. We all have different thoughts and feelings based on our background, culture, needs and desires. However, deep inside everyone on this planet is a place that is the same, the state of pure silence within. The unique quality of this silence is that my silence is the same as your silence. Silence is silence no matter who you are, no matter what the color of your skin, or where you live on this earth.

This silence, the source of thought, can be systematically experienced through the practice of TM. Scientific research shows that during TM, even from the first meditation, the brain produces increasingly coherent alpha waves. This distinct brain pattern corresponds to the state of silence, or inner wakefulness. This coherence spreads throughout the brain and is strongest in the prefrontal cortex—the seat of your brain's executive judgment.

A coherent brain operates from a state of unity. All the various specific neurons are united in this holistic experience of total brain functioning, the restful alertness present in the state of transcendental consciousness. This is a place where everyone can be united on the deepest level of life. When we are coherent and harmonious within, that coherence and unity will naturally spill out into the environment, creating more order and unity in our surroundings.

When women can meditate together and contact the field of pure consciousness, the unified field of infinite peace, this nourishing, uniting power is amplified many times in the environment. From this level of nature's functioning, we can radiate a powerful influence of harmony in our family, society, and nation.

While it is important to take immediate and strong actions on the outside to combat the present onslaught of racism, homophobia, and injustice, and continue to fight for equal rights and other issues facing women today, all these actions will be much more powerful if we can support them by accessing the deepest level within everyone. Einstein said that "Problems cannot be solved from the same level of consciousness that created them." Accessing more unified and unbounded levels of life will raise consciousness to a state where the solutions will emerge spontaneously.

At the United State of Women conference, Michelle Obama said "we stand stronger when we stand together." We will truly stand stronger when we stand united in our silence within. On the level of silence, we are "the Goddess" truly in connection with everyone, and from that level, we can create a beautiful, just, prosperous, and progressive world that supports all seven billion people in health and happiness.

Buddhist School for Girls in Thailand

Something special is happening in Thailand. Over 400 girls are blossoming like lotuses at the Dhammajarinee Witthaya School[8]—the first Buddhist boarding school for girls[9] from kindergarten through 12th grade.

In Thailand, boys who are poor or orphaned can go to a temple as a novice monk and receive an education. This has not been the case for girls. Seeing this inequality, Buddhist nuns founded Dhammajarinee Witthaya School. It is the only free Buddhist boarding school; girls from all over Thailand who come from impoverished families or have been orphaned attend the school.

Girls are the future of every nation. It is well documented that when girls receive a formal education, the nation achieves a higher standard of living and better health. Educated women improve the quality of life in their villages; their children are healthier and more educated. These young girls carry respect wherever they go and impart the importance of respecting others, particularly women.

Unfortunately, in many countries including Thailand, and especially in impoverished or stricken areas, young girls are vulnerable to AIDS, drug abuse, violence and exploitation. The Dhammajarinee Witthaya school provides a safe haven, as well as a quality education.

By providing a rigorous, modern academic curriculum along with Buddhist teachings, the school helps girls make better choices and achieve higher positions in society. They lead healthier lives, and become the future leaders of their communities. Because many of them have suffered past traumas, to reduce depression, anxiety, alienation, and fear the school includes yoga *asanas* and Transcendental Meditation as part of their daily routine.

Acharn Yai, a Buddhist nun and the principal of Dhammajarinee Witthaya School, says,

> The students learn TM at the beginning of the semester when they first arrive. Coming from different places, their behavior was quite aggressive, and they didn't pay attention to their studies. After learning meditation, they become more calm and settled. Their aggressive behavior decreases, their grades go up; they pay more attention to whatever we teach them. When they have inner happiness, they soak up whatever knowledge we give, unlike before.

It is beautiful to know that these young precious flowers of Thailand are blossoming into the fullness of who they are, and becoming enlightened leaders for their communities, Thailand, and the world.

SECTION 10

ENVIRONMENT

Inner Sustainability: A New Concept for Earth Day

As the world spins round and round, as the years go by, as governments have meeting after meeting, where do we stand with respect to taking care of our planet? Some moments it feels like the world is spinning out of control—tornadoes are bigger and hurricanes are more powerful. I had never even heard of the word *tsunami* before a few years ago. Now the weather patterns seem to be going crazy; there are more droughts, floods, and fires. The other night, when drifting to sleep, I was actually wondering whether I am going to leave this planet while the going is still good.

Giving up on Governments

Frankly, I have given up on government. I've concluded that it is up to each one of us as individuals to do what we can in our homes and communities. When we think of the whole world, cleaning up the environment seems too daunting, even out of the realm of possibility. One thing I have learned over the years is that if you can break a big problem down into smaller pieces and then take action steps every day to deal with the smaller problems, it is amazing how much can be accomplished.

Cities Are Taking Charge

The good news is that many mayors are doing just this in their communities; they are no longer waiting for Washington to solve their problems. For example, Philadelphia is vying to be the greenest city in the country as stated on the Mayor of Philadelphia sustainability website: "Let's make Philadelphia the Greenest City. That's the ambitious goal Mayor Michael A. Nutter has set for Philadelphia. Reaching it will be an opportunity to reposition and re-purpose Philadelphia as a city of the future."[1]

Greenest City in the World

Mother Nature Network[2] lists the current top 10 greenest cities in the United States with Portland, Oregon in the number one spot. The Green Optimistic[3] lists the top 10 greenest cities in the world; Portland is number five on this list. San Francisco was the only other U.S. city to make the global list. First place goes to Reykjavik in Iceland, a city completely powered by renewable energy, and governed largely by women.

The current buzzword in the green revolution is *sustainable*. Sustainable means conserving an ecological balance by avoiding depletion of natural resources. The 3 R's of the sustainability movement are reduce, reuse, and recycle.

Sustainability Within

The concept of sustainability can also apply directly to us as human beings. Can we become more sustainable within our own selves, and live longer, if we develop our consciousness? Just as we generate too much trash, and waste energy and resources in the environment, aren't we wasting energy when we are stressed and tired? Without renewing and replenishing our inner resources, such activity and exhaustion certainly is not sustainable: stress is a primary source of ill-health and often leads to hypertension, stroke, heart attack, and many other issues.

A field of pure energy and therefore pure sustainability lies within each of us. From there we can recycle ourselves and re-purpose our lives. Physicists have equated the transcendental level[4] with the unified field of natural law, which conducts the diversity of the entire universe without losing any energy. Our access to transcendental consciousness during meditation parallels this reality in the subjective experience. Through meditation[5] we tap into a level that will give us more and more energy and creativity.

Tapping into the Source of Infinite Energy

Maharishi talked about this exact point when he wrote in the *Science of Being and Art of Living*:

> The system of Transcendental Meditation, however, is the most effective way to bring the mind to the field of transcendental Being, where it will naturally acquire life-energy for performing any amount of hard work and for producing the most effective and desirable results. This drawing of energy from the field of Being is the most striking aspect of the art of living, for it brings the active life of the day-to-day world into communion with the source of limitless life—energy, power, intelligence, creativity and bliss.[6]

It is logical to conclude that if we are able to conserve more of our own energy and use it more wisely, we will be able to make sustainable choices for our environment as well. Therefore, the best thing we can do for the outer environment is to clean up the stress within our own internal environment. This is how each one of us can contribute on the deepest level to the sustainability of our planet.[7]

Global Interconnectedness—
Holistic Solutions

We live in an interconnected world, no doubt about it. Famines, epidemics, and other disasters have global impact; they reverberate around the world. News of a possible political or economic collapse in Somalia or Brazil, Greece or Uzbekistan, the U.S. or China, sets world stock markets spinning, since everyone recognizes we are now a global economy.

The Internet is fundamental in this interconnectedness. In an instant we hear the news of another country, find out the latest about our friends on Facebook, or look up information on virtually any topic via Google search.

One area in which the vision of interconnectedness is sorely lacking, however, is the field of politics, especially in regard to solving our nation's problems. For example, healthcare costs are skyrocketing in many countries. In the U.S., the epidemics of obesity and cardiovascular disease are threatening to bankrupt our healthcare system in the not-so-distant future.

Interconnectedness of Food and Health

Michelle Obama is to be congratulated for bringing more awareness to this issue. She has promoted many practical programs to solve the obesity crisis, such as Let's Move,[8] which emphasizes healthy eating and more physical activity.

However, the government currently subsidizes agrochemical industries,[9] particularly commodity crops like corn and soy. This artificially lowers the price of corn products, while at the same time making it more expensive to buy organic food. Because most corn is genetically engineered, expensive testing is necessary to ensure the purity of organic foods. In addition, organic foods receive little or no subsidies. Consequently, modified corn and soy products can be sold very cheaply on the market and are used in most processed food.

Unfortunately, because this "artificial food" is so much cheaper than healthy, fresh produce, people with limited incomes are forced to live on low-nutrition processed foods. This leads to obesity, diabetes, and other diet-related, potentially lethal problems. This situation is having a detrimental impact on lower-income families and a dramatic effect on the cost of healthcare. The connection between good food and better health is obvious, yet the government is failing to recognize this link, or at the very least, is acting slow as molasses to correct it.

Interconnectedness of People and the Environment

The devastating events of Hurricane Sandy[10] and Hurricane Katrina, and droughts in the western part of the U.S. have put global warming in the minds of many. We cannot divorce our environment from this theme of interconnectedness. The melting of the polar ice is slowly forcing us to see that changing one part of the delicate ecosphere affects the entire world. Unfortunately, most politicians, especially in the U.S., are still not acknowledging the science of global warming or seeing the importance of our interconnectedness with the environment.

Interconnectedness: Holistic Solutions

In the same way that many doctors are starting to see and treat the mind and body as a whole rather than treating isolated parts, governments need to see the interconnectedness between all their different departments, between nations, and between humanity and the environment.

The deepest level of interconnectedness is what physics calls the unified field of natural law, that level that governs the entire universe. Maharishi equates the unified field of natural law with the field of pure consciousness deep within every human being. The more people experience this unified field within themselves, the more they will naturally see outside themselves the connections that unite us all. Having a vision of interconnectedness helps prevent problems at their source.

"Interconnectedness" should be the government's new mantra. Leaders with this visionary outlook and the actual experience of interconnectedness are the only ones that deserve to have a place in guiding humanity to a more enlightened future.

Prince Charles—a Visionary Leader

Recently, my neighbor hosted Prince Charles[11] when he stopped in at George Washington's historic home in Mount Vernon during his trip to Washington, D.C. To prepare for his visit, she read his book *Harmony: A New Way of Looking at Our World.*[12] She was extremely impressed with the book and told me I would love it. When she went north for the summer, she gave me her copy.

Most of my knowledge of Prince Charles stems from reading *Royalty* magazine, flipping through image after image of royal dignitaries "at work," including Prince Charles repeatedly shaking hands with heads of state or at different social and charity events. Those articles were from the 1980s and 1990s when I was living abroad. I had read that Prince Charles was involved in organic farming and would bring his organic vegetables with him when traveling. In recent years, I have seen news of some of his outreach, especially his views on global warming. Before reading *Harmony*, however, I was unaware of the full extent of his involvement in so many innovative projects that promise to make a beneficial impact on our world.

Prince Charles is on a crusade: what he calls a "Sustainability Revolution." What amazes me about *Harmony*[13] is that everything Prince Charles favors and supports is on the same page as the teachings of Maharishi Mahesh Yogi. Most people know Maharishi as the guru who brought Transcendental Meditation to the world. Very few people know the full depth and breadth of Maharishi's vision and detailed designs to create a vastly better world.

There are many striking parallels between the principles Prince Charles sets forth in his book and Maharishi's teachings. To try to do them justice, I will segment this blog into three different parts.

Prince Charles—a Visionary Leader Part 1

The Age of Disconnection and Ideal Housing

Right from the first pages of *Harmony*, Prince Charles lays out the book's central theme: humankind needs a transformative change of perception. He explains that science boasts a great track record in discovering how things work, but is unable to explain the meaning of why they work. Philosophy, religion, and spirituality attempt to explain the *whys*—the *meaning behind* how things work.

Throughout his book, Prince Charles shows us how we have lost connection with those *whys*, and, more importantly, how we have lost connection with ourselves—to the "voice of the soul."[14]

Prince Charles describes how, in seventeenth-century Europe, western thinking took on a rather fragmented view of the world. As scholars and scientists probed into nature's functioning with an item-by-item approach to investigation, they began to lose the spiritual, holistic view of humanity's relationship with nature—a unified worldview that was prevalent in all ancient cultures. The lack of this holistic perception through which nature and people are viewed as integral to a grand whole is the basis of many of the problems we face today. Prince Charles calls this loss of wholeness the "Age of Disconnection."[15]

Maharishi shared this viewpoint, locating the cause of the piecemeal view of nature in the loss of the knowledge and direct experience of our own Self. This is Self with a capital "S," the "big" Self, the universal field of intelligence that underlies and pervades all life. The field of unity—the unified source of all expressions of diversity—has been identified by quantum physics as the unified field of natural law. Maharishi equated the unified field of all the laws of nature with the transcendental, deepest level of our Self.

When the mind starts identifying only with isolated laws of nature and loses connection with this unified "home" of all the laws of nature that lies within each of us, problems and disease can arise. In the Vedic language, this fragmentation is called *Pragyāparādh*—the "mistake of the intellect."

The technique of Transcendental Meditation, which Maharishi brought to the western world, is a direct, natural, and effortless way to reestablish our connection with the inner unity that lies within the silent depths of our Self.

Order in the Universe

In *Harmony*, Prince Charles explores the "sacred geometry" displayed in the architecture and art of the major ancient cultures. He explains: "The patterning that forms sacred geometry is derived from a very close observation of nature."[16] Ancient cultures understood that the outer order observable in the world is based on inner harmony, which is the very structure of nature itself. To access this higher ordered realm, we must activate the soul and draw upon its inner harmonious qualities.

Maharishi was fond of the following quote from the Yajur-Veda: *Yathā piṇde tathā brahmāṇde*—"As is the atom, so is the universe; as is the human body, so is the cosmic body." The entirety of the universe, including the human physiology, exhibits the same orderly patterns that are found at every level of nature's functioning.

Maharishi's unique contribution to the Vedic knowledge was in realizing the importance of the sequential, mathematical development of sound and silence present at the basis of creation. He especially highlighted the value of the "gap," the unexpressed foundational structure of nature. This unmanifest structure reveals itself at different stages of manifestation in DNA, cells, the human body, and the universe. When we understand and experience this structure, the "sacred geometry" of all life, it is possible to create outer structures that mirror, resonate with, and enhance our experience of the fundamental unity that connects us all.

The Architecture of Nature

Maharishi revived the knowledge of Sthāpatya Veda, the ancient science of architecture according to natural law, and called it Maharishi Vedic™ Architecture or Maharishi Vāstu®. Sthāpatya Veda prescribes specific mathematical principles for construction of buildings that reflect the orderliness of nature. The architecture of many of the world's oldest civilizations reflect principles and proportions similar to those found in the texts of Sthāpatya Veda.

Maharishi says:

Because the individual life is cosmic, everything about individual life should be in full harmony with Cosmic Life. Maharishi Vedic™ architecture gives dimensions, formulas, and orientations to the buildings that will provide cosmic harmony and support to the individual for his peace, prosperity, and good health—daily life in accord with Natural Law, daily life in the evolutionary direction.[17]

Prince Charles is involved in Sustainable Urbanism—ideal city planning that uses natural building materials and intelligently designed communities. He has worked on many low-income housing developments that enable residents to walk to their grocery stores and workplaces. Cars are kept on the outskirts to reduce air pollution. Trees and parks are planted throughout the towns to enhance air quality and beautification and the overall well-being of the people.

Maharishi spent hundreds of hours planning ideal housing developments[18]—what he called Vedic Garden Cities—based on Sthāpatya Veda. These developments use the same basic principles as Sustainable Urbanism, i.e., buildings can be designed in any style of architecture, but they should be symmetric to create a sense of balance. The use of nontoxic and natural building materials is pervasive. The communities are designed so that everyone can walk to work, have access to groceries, shops, and other vital daily activities.

One important element in Maharishi Vedic architecture that has not been considered in Sustainable Urbanism, however, is the emphasis on the orientation of the homes and office buildings, which should face due east or north.

Elements of Order

The main principles of Maharishi Vedic architecture[19] include directional orientation (on the grid, north-south-east-west), placement of rooms in relation to each other, and proportion and scale of the rooms. For example, the ancient texts go into detail about the placement of every room in the home based on the activity that it will house, including what areas are best for cooking, sleeping, eating, studying, eliminating waste, socializing, and meditating.

When buying a home, one does not usually think about how the path of the sun's light will hit the building throughout the day, or ask whether a house is properly placed on the grid—facing directly east, according to true, not magnetic, north. According to Maharishi Vedic architecture, having ample sunlight shining through the home goes a long way towards uplifting the inhabitants' spirits. I am sure everyone has experienced how depressing it is to be in a dreary home with very little natural light. Maharishi Vāstu homes are oriented to the east to take maximum advantage of the sun's nourishing light in the home throughout the day.

In addition to planning for the ideal orientation of homes and towns, Maharishi envisioned (and I am sure Prince Charles would also advocate this) that every community would have its own local organic farms.

As more people desire to live a sustainable, non-toxic lifestyle, and promote the future sustainability of our planet, green housing is a rapidly growing trend. Incorporating the precise directional and proportional elements of Sthāpatya Veda will add a powerful engine to the art and science of creating healthy homes!

Living in a home that is aligned with the sunrise helps us live our lives in greater harmony with natural law. As a result, our daily activity will spontaneously be more aligned with natural law, and our health will be better.

In Part 2, I discuss the relationship between the Age of Disconnection and the field of education.

Prince Charles—a Visionary Leader Part 2

The Age of Disconnection and Holistic Education

To help us understand how science was disconnected from the spiritual unity of life, Prince Charles describes in *Harmony* the major historical shifts in human thought over the past eight centuries. One of the prevailing assumptions of the great scholars and religious thinkers of thirteenth-century Europe and, preceding this, the Stoics of ancient Greece, Aristotle, and St. Thomas of Aquinas, was: "The creator was not separate from his creation. Instead, divinity was considered to be innate in the world and in us . . ."[20]

Fast forwarding to the seventeenth century, Prince Charles explains that, at this time, the authority of the Roman Catholic Church faced major challenges: "the growing trend towards humanism and the Protestantism that was questioning the supreme power invested in the Pope."[21]

He goes on to say that the Scientific Revolution caused people to begin thinking in a mechanistic way. This "reductive" approach separates out the different elements of an organism and examines the parts. Thus, over time, the definition of God changed from a divinity integrated in every part of creation to a Being that was separate from, and observing, nature. Prince Charles explains: ". . . as that happened, so Nature itself came to be seen more and more as an unpredictable force . . ."[22]

Universities of these earlier centuries had taught integrated knowledge—outer reality was understood as an external expression of what was inside—but, as science began to make a clean break from conventional religion, nature was understood as being outside of us, something we could conquer and control. Education began to reflect this separation of self and environment, inner and outer, and focused on separate bits of information rather than on connections. This marked the beginning of the modern industrial age.

A Return to Holistic Education

To ensure the sustainability of our planet, Prince Charles is actively involved in reestablishing a holistic approach to gaining knowledge, and applying it, through education. In *Harmony*, he cites several schools and university curricula that aim to have an integrated system of education.

In 2004, Prince Charles organized a new school, The Prince's School of Traditional Arts.[23] This school networks with other organizations and charities to support peace in troubled ethnic-minority communities, through such activities as student artwork and decoration for their schools' new faith centers.

The School of Traditional Arts focuses mainly on the arts, but also integrates art with math, geometry, and science so that children learn from a broad base. The children connect their lessons in math and science to different aspects of nature. Through this learning methodology, the students become aware of universal patterns in nature including those within their own bodies.

This educational approach is similar to Maharishi's Consciousness-Based Education.[24] In 1974, Maharishi established a flagship university, Maharishi University of Management[25] (MUM), which offers bachelors, masters, and doctoral degrees and is accredited by the North Central Association Higher Learning Commission. He also established the award-winning Maharishi School of the Age of Enlightenment,[26] which has students from preschool to twelfth grade. Both are located in Fairfield, Iowa, USA.

During their first year at MUM, students study all the major disciplines in the light of Maharishi Vedic Science. *Veda* means knowledge. Maharishi Vedic Science is the study, or knowledge, of your inner, infinite Self—the Self of the universe. The students and faculty practice Transcendental Meditation as part of their daily routine. In addition, students learn the universal principles of intelligence that are prevalent in every field of study and discover that all knowledge emerges from the unified field of consciousness.

Through Consciousness-based education, the students see the interconnectedness of every discipline, which is the fulfillment of the word "uni-versity;" "uni" refers to one and "versity" intimates diversity. They learn the unity at the heart of all diversity. They grow to feel at home with the knowledge they are studying in class and that they are imbibing through their growing familiarity with pure consciousness during practice of meditation. They soon realize that knowledge is structured in their own consciousness.

Most universities are information-based. As a consequence, students often feel completely separate from what they are learning, because there is nothing that links the pieces of knowledge to the knower. At MUM, students enjoy the learning process because it is all about their own Self. They connect with what they are studying on a deep level and gain energy and clarity of thinking through TM. This, in turn, helps them to focus and absorb more in class.

A popular area of study at MUM is the Sustainable Living Program. In 2012, the university completed construction of the most advanced Sustainable Living Center[27] in America. Students and faculty from surrounding colleges and universities come to visit MUM's Sustainable Living Department and see its amazing classroom building. The building is a hands-on teaching aid, demonstrating advanced green building techniques and materials. It is also built according to the principles of Maharishi Vedic Architecture.[28]

Prince Charles has worked towards a more sustainable world for years. In his book, he cites many secondary schools and colleges that are now teaching sustainable practices, especially in farming.

The approach to education that Prince Charles supports, as well as institutions of higher education like Maharishi University of Management, cultivate people who are able to see the *part* in terms of the *whole*. These students will be able to envision holistic solutions and have the knowledge and the drive to implement them.

I believe education is the key to creating a better world. Reconnecting students to their inner harmony and to the interconnectedness of all fields of knowledge is an essential and timely step to meeting the urgent needs of our precarious times.

Instead of living in an "Age of Disconnection," we can live in a new time of connectedness. We already see more connectivity worldwide through the Internet; adding the foundation of the unified field of natural law and the inner experience of pure consciousness into education will create a new "Age of Connection and Harmony." I will elaborate in Part 3 how this integrated approach is applied to natural healthcare and the environment.

Prince Charles—a Visionary Leader Part 3
The Age of Disconnection, Holistic Health, and Environmental Awareness

The disconnect between nature and our industrial, tech-based age is woefully obvious, as evidenced by the thousands of chemicals, pesticides, and genetically modified organisms (GMOs) prevalent in our food and environment. Consequently, we face the devastating effects of climate change, water pollution, demise of honeybee colonies and other species, and an unhealthy food supply.

Solutions on the Horizon

In 2010, Prince Charles launched an initiative called Start[29] to encourage people to live sustainably. Through Start he is working with schools and corporations around the world to promote a sustainability mindset through the use of positive messages and practices rather than a doom-and-gloom approach.

In a similar vein, Maharishi encouraged organic farming to improve the health and self-sufficiency of all peoples. He strongly advised against GMOs, which he viewed as one of the biggest threats to the integrity of our planet.

In the field of health, Prince Charles supports many foundations and projects promoting natural holistic approaches to healthcare.

Maharishi also spent years working with traditional doctors in India to re-establish the lost science of Ayurveda in its completeness. Ayurveda—*Veda* means knowledge and *ayu* means lifespan—is the knowledge of how to live a long, healthy life. Ayurveda emphasizes the mind–body connection and treating the body as a whole. It offers ways to maintain balance in the physiology, to prevent disease, and to treat chronic disorders with natural herbs and medicines.

There are several Maharishi AyurVeda (MAV) health clinics around the world, including The Raj, which has come to be known as the premier Ayurvedic health spa in the United States. The Maharishi AyurVeda clinics report remarkable success in treating chronic disease without the harmful side effects of allopathic medication. There is an accelerating trend towards alternative treatments, such as programs that address the underlying cause of disease, and regaining health through a balanced diet, natural supplements, and an appropriate exercise regime.

I have only touched briefly upon the many far-reaching, visionary programs in the fields of architecture, education, healthcare, and sustainability in which Prince Charles is actively participating and have provided just a glimpse of the Vedic knowledge that Maharishi revived. It is encouraging that these practical programs to create a better world are rapidly gaining acceptance, as are hundreds of other recent innovative projects with similar objectives initiated by other visionary leaders.

Unfortunately, we rarely hear about these unique programs because editors, journalists, and newscasters are paid to broadcast what the media moguls believe the public wants most to hear, i.e., violent, shocking news and celebrity gossip. With the terrorist attacks in Paris and Brussels, shootings in the U.S., the pervasive worldwide threat from ISIS, and the ravaging effects of global warming,[30] I obviously get concerned.

The Nature of Evolution

Although the situation in the world seems precarious, I remain an optimist. A silent revolution of innovative solutions to the world's most challenging problems is taking place beneath the surface chaos. A rapid spiritual evolution, or revolution, is also unfolding as more people worldwide practice meditation to experience the universal harmony of nature within themselves.

The spiritual awakening that is underway is evidenced by the Yoga centers found on street corners around the world. The essential meaning of Yoga is union of the individual with the cosmic. When we realize that our deepest nature within is the deepest cosmic nature of all creation, we will no longer be able to harm the earth—nor anyone else. We will come to see that destroying any part of our earth is damaging our own life breath, which the wind sweetly gives us.

There is a rapidly growing movement of people who want alternative, holistic healthcare and who embrace nature's harmony within themselves and in their surroundings. This is beautifully articulated in *Harmony*.[31] More people are against GMOs, or at least in favor of labeling GMO products. We are buying local produce and favoring organic,[32] and "becoming the change we want to see in the world." Hundreds of schools around the world now have their own organic gardens to feed their students.

In *Maharishi's Master Plan to Create Heaven on Earth*, Maharishi states:

When the connectedness of individual life with Cosmic Life is damaged, intelligence remains disconnected from its own Cosmic Value. It grows like a bud without flowering and without the ability to spread its fragrance and glorify the whole atmosphere. This is the deplorable state of life imposed upon mankind through Modern Science-based education.[33]

As Prince Charles similarly states in *Harmony*: "Creation is a living presence, woven into the fabric of everything, and their [primary cultures] communion with its presence offers knowledge of the world."[34]

As both Maharishi and Prince Charles point out, our inherent harmony or unity with nature can and should be restored for wholeness of life. It is obvious that we have a long way to go, but there is nothing so powerful as an idea whose time has come.

Sustainability, spirituality, and the experience of interconnectedness of all life that is born from that spirituality, are ideas and realities whose time surely has come!

GMOs: Are We Crossing the Tipping Point?

Recently I have seen many references in the media that show a dramatic shift in positive trends regarding genetically modified organisms (GMO). Hellman's Mayonnaise is the latest brand going non-GMO, and Chipotle[35] is the first national food chain that is going non-GMO. One of the largest baby formula makers, Similac, recently said that they would start offering a non-GMO version of their formula. Pizza Hut and Taco Bell[36] are removing all artificial ingredients from their products, with the CEO of Pizza Hut saying that he is making the changes in response to customer demand.

Big businesses invest a great deal in making their desires known to our government. In order to create change we as citizens must use whatever means available to inform our representatives in government of our own desires for health and wellness.

Governments Are Getting on Board

Vermont is the first state to require the labeling[37] of genetically modified food. Even though the majority of Vermonters want the labeling, big business is now taking the issue to court. If Vermont wins the case, then many states will follow suit. Maine and Connecticut also have the same laws, but will only implement them if Vermont wins the case. Ben and Jerry's has gone non-GMO and its founders are campaigning in Washington, D.C. to encourage government support for labeling GMO-laced foods.

Musician-composer Neil Young just wrote a song called "Rock Starbucks." A line in the song is "Yeah, I want a cup of coffee, but I don't want a GMO." Young is campaigning to boycott Starbucks until they cut their ties with Monsanto and proceed into the future GMO-free.

Countries and Regions Ban GMOs and Glyphosate

More and more countries are going GMO-free and/or glyphosate-free. Glyphosate is a herbicide that has been linked to cancer-causing toxins.[38] Sri Lanka[39] and the Netherlands are the latest two countries to ban glyphosate usage, joining Mexico, Russia, South Africa, France, Chile, and Brazil.[40]

There is a growing list of countries that have banned the sale of seeds or substances containing GMOs. Almost every day I see a new Facebook post stating that another region or nation is banning GMOs. Public outcry is growing against GMO crops.

As I write this article I see two new posts on my Facebook feed. One states that a judge upheld Jackson County, Oregon's ban on GMO crops; the other says Hungary has just announced they are to be the first EU nation to ban GMOs. The Deputy State Secretary of Hungary said he is convinced this is the only way to ensure families will have access to safe foods.

These changes are a direct result of citizens demanding healthier food. Hopefully, this attitude and policy position will snowball and gather momentum such that every person on the planet can enjoy safe, healthy food. It is a race against time—to stop the spread of GMOs and ban harmful pesticides.

We the people have the power, and must be bold in maximizing that power. We have to reclaim our democracy and put people first, not just the wealthy few or the corporate interests. To do so we have to vote with our wallets! People, we are on a roll. Let's win this race now!

SECTION 11

GIFTS OF NATURE

Mango Season Has Arrived

Heaven, pure nectar, sumptuous, mouth-watering bliss! This is what I feel as the soft texture of mango enlivens my taste buds. I savor each bite of the creamy texture as piece by piece effortlessly slides down and fills my whole Being with ecstasy! Mango season is finally here, yay! I have been impatiently counting the days since this time last year.

Without a doubt, mango is my favorite fruit. When the season comes, I have mango smoothies, mango chutneys, mango ice cream, mango sherbet, mango crumble, and best of all; a plain, freshly cut mango.

Three years ago, I discovered an organic mango orchard in Delray Beach, Florida off Seacrest Boulevard, called Truly Tropical.[1] They offer over 50 varieties of mango. I never knew so many types existed, and every kind is delicious. It is a pure delight to discern the subtle, unique tastes of the different varieties.

Driving into the mango orchard, one sees hundreds of saffron colored mangos, dangling from the trees like golden droplets ready to fall to the ground. It is paradise for mango lovers.

As with any organic fruit or vegetable, mangos grown locally and in season, such as those that have freshly fallen to the ground, will be healthier, sweeter, and usually cheaper than those that are shipped in.

"Foods lose flavor just as they lose moisture when they are held. Fresh, locally harvested foods have their full, whole flavors intact, which they release to us when we eat them," explains Susan Herrmann Loomis, owner of On Rue Tatin Cooking School in France and the author of numerous cookbooks. "Foods that are chilled and shipped lose flavor at every step of the way—chilling cuts their flavor, transport cuts their flavor, being held in warehouses cuts their flavor."[2]

According to Brian Halweil, author of *Eat Here: Homegrown Pleasures in a Global Supermarket*, "If you harvest something early so that it can endure a long distance shipping experience, it's not going to have the full complement of nutrients it might have had."[3]

Transporting produce sometimes requires irradiation, which means ionizing radiation is applied to the food to kill microorganisms. In addition, preservatives are sprayed to protect the produce, which is subsequently refrigerated during the trip.

Fortunately, mangos are a healthy fruit and contain 20 vitamins and minerals. Studies suggest that mangos decrease the risk of obesity, diabetes, and heart disease.[4] Eating mangos also promotes a healthy complexion and even weight loss.

How can a piece of fruit that tastes so good have so many health benefits? Maybe it is better not to analyze this question. Just enjoy the bursts of bliss that result from eating this sweet gift from nature and count your blessings that you are fortunate to experience the heavenly joy of fresh, ripe mangos while on this earth.

Papaya and Other Exotic Fruits

I could spend my life trying to explain how a papaya tastes, but you would never know until you tasted it yourself. My experience of eating one is a burst of mouth-watering bliss. Can one reduce the reality of heaven to the oral cavity? I would say yes, at least for a few moments!

I was fortunate to wake up recently in Kauai, Hawaii, to an exotic array of fruits—coconuts, papayas, mangos, lychees, tangerines, noni, guavas, pineapples, and rambutans to name a few. If any of these fruits do not generate a wave of gastronomical bliss, I don't know what else will. I have never enjoyed waking up so eager to have breakfast. What a way to start a day!

All day long I would hydrate myself with coconut water, which refreshed and revived me after an afternoon of running around. Fresh coconut water is the liquid inside the coconut. Coconut water is a sumptuous delight that can put one into a state of temporary rapture. As the cool, light liquid slides down your throat, you can feel its refreshment as it is being absorbed by every cell of your body.

Each of the fruits on the island has an abundance of health benefits and is nourishing to the physiology. They are packed with vitamins and minerals such as potassium, magnesium, copper, and cytokinins that reduce the risk of breast cancer, reduce inflammation, and protect the heart.

Meeting the people of Kauai, I am touched with their profound respect for the land. They call themselves Keiki kam o'aina—children of the land. They believe that nature feeds man and man watches over nature in return.

I personally feel a wave of gratitude to Mother Nature and the beautiful land of Hawaii for providing such an extensive array of incredible health-giving fruits that are so euphorically delicious while at the same time have many benefits for one's well-being.

Aloha!

Gwyneth Paltrow and Chocolate Mousse

As the creamy smooth chocolate pudding filled my mouth, my taste buds woke up and savored every bite of the rich buttery texture. I never would have guessed that avocado formed the basis of this pudding! The chocolate mousse was from a recipe in Gwyneth Paltrow's new cookbook, *It's All Easy.*[5]

Ms. Paltrow was doing a book signing at my family's club in East Hampton at a lady's night dinner for over 150 women. The sun setting with a mountain of pink clouds over the ocean formed the backdrop of her presentation. She started her talk by saying how wonderful it is for women to get together. Rather than giving a straight lecture she invited questions, opening it to any topic the crowd was interested in asking her. Questions ranged from the importance of using non-toxic products on one's body, to balancing work and home life, to her website Goop.com,[6] to her acting career. One of the ladies even asked about Paltrow's ex-husband Chris Martin. She said they were very good friends, and that, in fact, he was at her house at the moment taking care of their children.

Gwyneth answered every question with candor and humor. I was particularly impressed with how knowledgeable she was about how disruptive chemicals in skin-care products can be to the hormonal and endocrine systems.

Someone asked Gwyneth if she would sing a song from one of her movies. She fearlessly obliged and perfectly sang a verse of the song, "Cruisin'" that she sang with Huey Lewis in the movie *Duets*.

As Gwyneth started her book signing, the buffet dinner also began. Every delicious dish was made from recipes in her cookbook. The menu was burrata with thinly sliced cucumber on top, crispy polenta with sauce, mixed roasted vegetables with avocado, roasted chicken, seared scallops with vegetables, and chocolate mousse for dessert.

As a vegetarian, I was happy there were enough dishes for me to eat. The burrata with shaved cucumber was elegant to look at and refreshing to eat on a summer's evening. The roasted vegetables were crisp and savory as was the polenta.

My friend sitting next to me told me, "The chicken was delicious and simple—no odd combination of flavors, which is so common nowadays. It was golden on the outside and very tender, moist, and well-cooked on the inside. Yummy!"

The highlight for me was the chocolate mousse. Everybody at my table was "oohing" and "ahhing" during every bite. Everyone was as surprised as I was to learn that avocado was in it. I came away that evening with a renewed appreciation for Gwyneth Paltrow. I loved her easy, fun-loving nature and her desire to bring a non-toxic, better quality of life to others through her lifestyle website, Goop.

My 90-year-old mother and I were going through Gwyneth's cookbook last night before going to bed. There were many ingredients she had never heard of such as acai, chia seeds, kimchi, veganaise, garam masala, tamari, hemp seeds, coconut sugar, wasabi powder, and much more. We both look forward to trying many new recipes in Gwyneth Paltrow's book. The first ones I want to try are the beet chips, ginger chia pudding, and of course, the chocolate mousse!

May—Florida at Its Best

May is my favorite month in Florida. The winter crowds have gone and a quieter, settled feeling descends upon the small coastal town where I live. Although the weather starts to get warmer, the heat does not yet cast its July and August oppression.

Have you ever noticed how happy everyone is at the beach, especially the children? The ocean is pure bliss for them as their laughter echoes everywhere. In May in Florida, the ocean is a perfect temperature, like a warm bath. Diving into the ocean washes away any tension and restores you to a state of peaceful joy.

The ocean is like a meditation. The aqua clear water calms and the lapping waves soothe. The vast expanse of the ocean and the infinite sky above are like the unbounded expanse of the transcendent in the state of pure Being.

Watching the sun cast its sparkles on the sea is watching divinity dancing. It is literally like watching the same divinity that dances within when consciousness wakes up and observes its own shimmering nature.

Sunrises over the ocean are ever changing, ever new. The sun peeking over the horizon is always a thrilling and magical moment. These blessed few minutes make me feel so grateful to be alive to witness this beauty. Watching the sunrise is a perfect way to start the day.

The balmy breeze and the sound of the palm trees rustling in the evening are sounds that soothe my soul. Walking on the beach at night and seeing the small flashes of light from the multitude of boats on the sea in the distance and the moon above are also precious moments to capture.

I love the sunshine state of Florida, especially during the month of May.

ACKNOWLEDGEMENTS

I would like to thank my publisher, Gary Wilson, for suggesting and strongly encouraging me to create this book of all the blogs I have written since *The Transcendental Meditation Technique and the Journey of Enlightenment* was published.

I would also like to thank Nicole Windenberger for her editing skills and continued persistence in making the articles and references as complete as possible, my webmaster, Eric Carter-Spurio, for his patience and computer and project management skills in bringing these articles to the public, and Robert Johnson for his contribution to the formatting and design of the text.

A big thank you to all the readers of my blogs for sending in their thoughtful comments and words of appreciation.

My friends on the Mother Divine Program[SM] are my greatest source of inspiration and support. Thank you for dedicating your lives to bringing peace to the world.

I also want to thank my mother for always being there for me, all my siblings, who have made me a stronger person, and my nieces, nephews, great-nieces and great-nephews who bring so much love and joy to my life.

NOTES

The Power of Transcendence

Huffington Post Blog. (2014, December 3). http://www.huffingtonpost.com/ann
-purcell/the-power-of-transcendenc_b_6237966.html

1. Quoted in Craig Pearson, *The Supreme Awakening: Experiences of
   Enlightenment Throughout Time—And How You Can Cultivate Them*
   (Fairfield, Iowa, USA: MUM Press, 2013), 168. Originally from Anwar Sadat,
   In Search of Identity: An Autobiography (Harper and Row: 1977).

2. Pearson, *The Supreme Awakening*, 168-169.

3. Smith, Emily. 2014. "Meditation sessions a hit in dysfunctional Congress."
   Page Six, October 25, 2014. http://pagesix.com/2014/10/25/
   meditation-sessions-become-a-hit-in-dysfunctional-congress/.

4. Bendery, Jennifer. 2013. "Amid The Chaos Of Capitol Hill, Tim Ryan Offers
   Reprieve With Quiet Time Caucus." Huffington Post, July 25, 2013. http://
   www.huffingtonpost.com/2013/07/25/tim-ryan-quiet-time-caucus_n
   _3653247.html.

5. Do You Yoga. n.d. "The British Parliament Stops to Meditate." Accessed
   July 8, 2017. https://www.doyouyoga.com/the-british-parliament-stops
   -to-meditate/.

Section 1—Love

Fathoming the Infinite Depths of Love

Enlightenment is for Everyone Blog. (2013, October 13). http://enlightenment
foreveryone.com/2013/10/17/fathoming-the-infinite-depths-of-love/

1. Maharishi Mahesh Yogi. *Love and God*. Available at MUM Press: http://
   www.mumpress.com/maharishi-books/love-and-god.html.

2. Maharishi Mahesh Yogi, *Love and God* (Oslo, Norway: Spiritual
   Regeneration Movement, 1965), 13-17.

3. Ibid., 20.

4. Ibid., 21.

5. Enlightenment is for Everyone. n.d. "Maharishi Mahesh Yogi." Accessed July 8, 2017. http://enlightenmentforeveryone.com/maharishi-mahesh-yogi/.

6. Maharishi Mahesh Yogi, *Love and God*, 21.

Love and Enlightenment

Huffington Post Blog. (2013, October 7). http://www.huffingtonpost.com/ann-purcell/love-enlightenment_b_4038285.html

7. Gunnar, Megan R., Mary C. Larson, Louise Hertsgaard, Michael L. Harris and Laurie Brodersen. 1992. "The Stressfulness of Separation among Nine-Month-Old Infants: Effects of Social Context Variables and Infant Temperament." *Child Development* 63, no. 2 (April): 290–303. https://doi.org/10.2307/1131479. https://www.ncbi.nlm.nih.gov/pubmed/1611934.

Additional Resources:

Hertsgaard, Louise, Megan Gunnar, Martha Farrell Erickson and Melissa Nachmias. 1995. "Adrenocortical Responses to the Strange Situation in Infants with Disorganized/Disoriented Attachment Relationships." *Child Development* 66, no. 4 (August): 1100–1106. https://doi.org/10.2307/1131801. http://onlinelibrary.wiley.com/wol1/doi/10.1111/j.1467-8624.1995.tb00925.x/abstract.

Center on the Developing Child at Harvard University. 2012. *The Science of Neglect: The Persistent Absence of Responsive Care Disrupts the Developing Brain: Working Paper 12.* http://www.developingchild.harvard.edu.

8. Enlightenment is for Everyone. n.d. "Enlightenment." http://enlightenmentforeveryone.com/enlightenment/.

9. Maharishi Mahesh Yogi, *Love and God*, 14.

10. Ibid., 19.

A Moment of Pure Love

Enlightenment is for Everyone Blog. (2015, April 20). http://enlightenmentforeveryone.com/2015/04/20/a-moment-of-pure-love/

Section 2—Creativity

Transcendence and the Creative Process

Huffington Post Blog. (2015, October 28). http://www.huffingtonpost.com/ann
-purcell/transcendence-and-the-cre_b_8409820.html

1. Abbott, Jim. 2014. "Paul McCartney Talks Music at Rollins College."
   Orlando Sentinel, October 30, 2014. http://www.orlandosentinel.com/
   entertainment/os-paul-mccartney-jim-abbott-20141030-column.html.

2. Roger Ebert, *Life Itself: A Memoir* (New York: Grand Central Publishing,
   2011), 4.

3. Arthur M. Abell, *Talks with Great Composers* (Philosophical Library, Inc.,
   c1955, 1987; reprint, New York: Carol Publishing Group, 1994), 86.

4. David Lynch, *Catching the Big Fish: Meditation, Consciousness, and Creativity*
   (New York: Penguin Group, 2006), 27-28.

The Blank Canvas

Enlightenment is for Everyone Blog. (2017, February 13). http://enlightenment
foreveryone.com/2017/02/13/creativity-consciousness/

Music for Change

Enlightenment is for Everyone Blog. (2012, August 8). http://enlightenmentfor
everyone.com/?s=music+for+change

5. Playing for Change: http://playingforchange.com

6. Johnson, Mark. Interview by Max Foster. *Connect the World*, CNN, April 20,
   2011. Accessed August 2012. http://edition.cnn.com/videos/showbiz/2011/
   04/20/cotd.mark.johnson.cnn.

7. Playing For Change. "Stand By Me | Playing For Change | Song Around
   The World." Youtube video, 5:27, from the documentary, "Playing
   For Change: Peace Through Music." Posted November 6, 2008.
   https://www.youtube.com/watch?v=Us-TVg4OExM.

8. Whitacre, Eric. 2011. "A virtual choir 2,000 voices strong | Eric Whitacre."
   Filmed March 1, 2011 at TED2011, LongBeach Performing Arts Center,
   CA, USA. Video, 14:34. https://www.ted.com/talks/eric_whitacre_a_virtual
   _choir_2_000_voices_strong.

9. EricWhitacreVEVO. "Eric Whitacre—Eric Whitacre's Virtual Choir 2.0,
   'Sleep'." Youtube video, 9:30. The 2011 Virtual Choir video includes 2052
   performances of 'Sleep' from 1752 singers in 58 countries, individually
   recorded and uploaded to YouTube between September 2010 and January

2011. Posted April 6, 2011. https://www.youtube.com/
watch?v=6WhWDCw3Mng.

10. Playing For Change. "One Love | Playing For Change | Song Around The
World." Youtube video, 5:07, from the documentary "Playing For Change:
Peace Through Music," a rendition of the legendary Bob Marley song
"One Love" with Keb' Mo' and Manu Chao. Posted February 5, 2009.
https://www.youtube.com/watch?v=4xjPODksIo8.

11. USA for Africa. "We are the World." Audio, 7:14. Originally released
March 7, 1985. A&M Recording Studios, Los Angeles, CA. https://en
.wikipedia.org/wiki/We_Are_the_World#USA_for_Africa_musicians.
Accessed online: MichaelJacksonFM. "Michael Jackson: We Are The World
(Official Music Video)." Youtube video, 8:00. Posted July 7, 2009. https://
www.youtube.com/watch?v=cW_1YAYQK9g.

12. Wearetheworld. "We Are The World 25 For Haiti—Official Video."
Youtube video, 8:32. 25th anniversary recording of "We are the World"
featuring over 80 artists and performers to benefit the Haitian earthquake
relief efforts and the rebuilding of Haiti. Posted February 12, 2010.
https://www.youtube.com/watch?v=Glny4jSciVI.

What Inspired My Book about Enlightenment?

Enlightenment is for Everyone Blog. (2015, April 28). http://enlightenment
foreveryone.com/2015/04/28/what-inspired-my-book-about-enlightenment/

13. Enlightenment is for Everyone, "Enlightenment."

Section 3—Health and Well-Being

Stress: Your Worst Enemy

Huffington Post Blog. (2013, December 18). http://www.huffingtonpost.com/
ann-purcell/stress-your-worst-enemy_b_4427520.html

1. Maharishi Mahesh Yogi, *On The Bhagavad-Gita: A New Translation and
Commentary* (Baltimore: Penguin Books Inc., 1967), 292. (6:5)

2. Transcendental Meditation for Women Professionals. n.d. "Scientific
Research." http://tmwomenprofessionals.org/scientific-research/.

3. "How stress influences disease: Study reveals inflammation as the
culprit." Science Daily. April 2, 2012. Source: Carnegie Mellon University.
https://www.sciencedaily.com/releases/2012/04/120402162546.htm.
See also: Cohen, Sheldon, Denise Janicki-Deverts, William J. Doyle,

Gregory E. Miller, Ellen Frank, Bruce S. Rabin, and Ronald B. Turner. 2012. "Chronic stress, glucocorticoid receptor resistance, inflammation, and disease risk." *Proceedings of the National Academy of Sciences of the United States of America* 109, no. 16 (April): 5995–5999. http://doi.org/10.1073/pnas.1118355109. http://www.pnas.org/content/109/16/5995.

4. Huffington, Arianna. 2013. "Redefining Success: Takeaways From Our Third Metric Conference." Huffington Post Blog. June 14, 2013. http://www .huffingtonpost.com/arianna-huffington/redefining-success-take away_b_3444007.html.

5. Enlightenment: http://enlightenmentforeveryone.com/enlightenment/

Social Anxiety Disorder—a Solution

Enlightenment is for Everyone Blog. (2016, March 14). http://enlightenment foreveryone.com/2016/03/14/social-anxiety-disorder-solution/

6. University of Texas Counseling and Mental Health Center. n.d. "Anxiety." Accessed March 2016. https://cmhc.utexas.edu/anxiety.html.

7. Anxiety and Depression Association of America. n.d. "Social Anxiety Disorder." Accessed March 2016. https://adaa.org/understanding -anxiety/social-anxiety-disorder.

8. Mayo Clinic. n.d. "Social anxiety disorder (social phobia): Symptoms and causes." Accessed March 2016. http://www.mayoclinic.org/diseases -conditions/social-anxiety-disorder/basics/causes/con-20032524.

9. Maharishi Mahesh Yogi, *Bhagavad-Gita*, 293. (6:6)

10. Mercola, Joseph. 2016. "Anxiety Drug Overdoses in U.S. Hit Record Levels." Mercola. March 10, 2016. https://articles.mercola.com/sites/articles/ archive/2016/03/10/anxiety-drug-overdose.aspx.

11. Social Anxiety Institute. n.d. "Why CBT Works for Social Anxiety Disorder." https://socialanxietyinstitute.org/why-cbt-works-social -anxiety-disorder.

12. Rosenthal, Joshua Z., Sarina Grosswald, Richard Ross, Norman Rosenthal. 2011. "Effects of Transcendental Meditation in Veterans of Operation Enduring Freedom and Operation Iraqi Freedom With Posttraumatic Stress Disorder: A Pilot Study." *Military Medicine* 176, no. 6 (June): 626–630. doi: 10.7205/MILMED-D-10-00254. http://military medicine.amsus.org/doi/pdf/10.7205/MILMED-D-10-00254.

Operation Warrior Wellness and the Resilient Warrior program: David Lynch Foundation. n.d. "Operation Warrior Wellness:

building resilience and healing the hidden wounds of war."
https://www.davidlynchfoundation.org/veterans.html.

TM for Veterans: Overcoming Trauma, Building Resilience. n.d.
"Research on TM and PTSD." https://tmforveterans.org/research-on-tm
-and-ptsd/.

Enlightened Health Care—Self-Care

Enlightenment is for Everyone Blog. (2013, February 14). http://enlightenment
foreveryone.com/2013/02/14/enlightened-health-care/

13. Bradley, Linda. 2015. "10 Ways to Put Your Doctor Out of Business." Black
Health Matters. September 14, 2015. http://www.blackhealth
matters.com/our-health/general-health/linda-d-bradley-m-d-10-ways-to
-put-your-doctor-out-of-business/.

14. Barrow, Becky. 2011. "Stress 'is top cause of workplace sickness' and is so
widespread it's dubbed the 'Black Death of the 21st century'." *Mailonline*,
October 5, 2011. http://www.dailymail.co.uk/health/article-2045309/Stress
-Top-cause-workplace-sickness-dubbed-Black-Death-21st-century.html
#ixzz4mjQZcoE7.

15. Schneider, Robert H., Clarence E. Grim, Maxwell V. Rainforth, Theodore
Kotchen, Sanford I. Nidich, Carolyn Gaylord-King, John W. Salerno, et al.
2012. "Stress Reduction in the Secondary Prevention of Cardiovascular
Disease: Randomized, Controlled Trial of Transcendental Meditation
and Health Education in Blacks." *Circulation: Cardiovascular Quality and
Outcomes* 5, no. 6 (November): 750-758. https://doi.org/10.1161/CIRCOUT
COMES.112.967406. http://circoutcomes.ahajournals.org/content/5/6/750.

16. Blue, Laura. 2012. "Strongest Study Yet Shows Meditation Can Lower Risk
of Heart Attack and Stroke." *Time*, November 14, 2012. http://healthland
.time.com/2012/11/14/mind-over-matter-strongest-study-yet-shows
-meditation-can-lower-risk-of-heart-attack-and-stroke/.

17. Rosenthal, Norman. "Norman Rosenthal, M.D. on Transcendental
Meditation." Youtube video, 1:36. Posted by "Transcendental Meditation,"
April 27, 2010. https://www.youtube.com/watch?v=10XeslMRbiw.

18. Girod, Chris, Sue Hart, and Scott Weltz. "Healthcare costs for the
typical American family will exceed $25,000 in 2016. Who cooked up this
expensive recipe?" Millman Medical Index. May 2016. http://us.milliman
.com/uploadedFiles/insight/Periodicals/mmi/2016-milliman-medical-index
.pdf.

19. Herron, Robert E. 2011. "Changes in Physician Costs Among High-Cost
Transcendental Meditation Practitioners Compared With High-

Cost Nonpractitioners Over 5 Years." *American Journal of Health Promotion* 26, no. 1 (September-October): 56-60. doi: 10.4278/ajhp.100729-ARB-258. https://www.ncbi.nlm.nih.gov/pubmed/21879945.

Transcendental Meditation to Reduce High Blood Pressure

Enlightenment is for Everyone Blog. (2013, May 21). http://enlightenment foreveryone.com/2013/05/21/transcendental-meditation-to-reduce-high -blood-pressure/

20. Brook, Robert D., Lawrence J. Appel, Melvyn Rubenfire, Gbenga Ogedegbe, John D. Bisognano, William J. Elliott, Flavio D. Fuchs, et al. 2013. "Beyond Medications and Diet: Alternative Approaches to Lowering Blood Pressure: A Scientific Statement From the American Heart Association." *Hypertension* 61, no. 6 (June): 1360-1383. https://doi.org/10.1161/HYP .0b013e318293645f. http://hyper.ahajournals.org/content/early/2013/04/22/ HYP.0b013e318293645f.

21. Mozzafarian, Dariush, Emelia J. Benjamin, Alan S. Go, Donna K. Arnett, Michael J. Blaha, Mary Cushman, Sarah de Ferranti, et al. 2015. "Heart Disease and Stroke Statistics-2015 Update: a report from the American Heart Association." *Circulation* 131, no. 4 (January): e29-e322. Table 9-1. https://doi.org/10.1161/CIR.000000000000152. http://circ.ahajournals .org/content/131/4/e29.long#sec-156.

22. Heidenreich, Paul A., Justin G. Trogdon, Olga A. Khavjou, Javed Butler, Kathleen Dracup, Michael D. Ezekowitz, Eric Andrew Finkelstein, et al. 2011. "Forecasting the Future of Cardiovascular Disease in the United States: A Policy Statement From the American Heart Association." *Circulation* 123, no. 8 (March): 933-944. https://doi.org/10.1161/CIR .0b013e31820a55f5. http://circ.ahajournals.org/content/early/2011/01/24/CIR .0b013e31820a55f5.

23. Herron, Robert E. 2012. "Can TM Save Medicare from Bankruptcy?" TM Blog. July 19, 2012. http://www.tm.org/blog/news/can-tm-save-medicare -and-medicaid/.

24. National Institutes of Health: https://www.nih.gov

25. Walton, Kenneth G., Robert H. Schneider, and Sanford Nidich. 2004. "Review of Controlled Research on the Transcendental Meditation Program and Cardiovascular Disease: Risk Factors, Morbidity, and Mortality." *Cardiology in Review* 12, no. 5 (September): 262-266. doi: 10 .1097/01.crd.0000113021.96119.78. https://www.ncbi.nlm.nih.gov/pmc/ articles/PMC2211376/#.

26. Nidich, Sanford, Maxwell V. Rainforth, David A.F. Haaga, John Hagelin, John W. Salerno, Fred Travis, Melissa Tanner, et al. 2009. "A Randomized Controlled Trial on Effects of the Transcendental Meditation Program on Blood Pressure, Psychological Distress, and Coping in Young Adults." *American Journal of Hypertension* 22, no. 12 (December): 1326-1331. doi: 10.1038/ajh.2009.184. https://www.ncbi.nlm.nih.gov/pubmed/19798037.

27. Dillbeck, Michael. 1982. "Meditation and Flexibility of Visual Perception and Verbal Problem Solving." *Memory & Cognition* 10, no. 3 (May): 207–215. https://doi.org/10.3758/BF03197631. https://link.springer.com/article/10.3758/BF03197631.

28. Travis, Frederick. 1979. "The Transcendental Meditation Technique and Creativity: A Longitudinal Study of Cornell University Undergraduates." *The Journal of Creative Behavior* 13, no. 3 (September): 169–180. doi:10.1002/j.2162-6057.1979.tb00203.x. http://onlinelibrary.wiley.com/doi/10.1002/j.2162-6057.1979.tb00203.x/abstract.

29. Wallace, Robert K., Michael Dillbeck, Eliha Jacobe, Beth Harrington. 1982. "The Effects of the Transcendental Meditation Program on the Aging Process." *International Journal of Neuroscience* 16, no. 1 (February): 53-58. http://dx.doi.org/10.3109/00207458209147602. https://www.ncbi.nlm.nih.gov/pubmed/6763007.

30. Purcell, Ann. 2013. "Enlightened Health Care—Self-Care: Meditation to Reduce Stress." Enlightenment is for Everyone blog. February 14, 2013. http://enlightenmentforeveryone.com/2013/02/14/enlightened-health-care/.

31. Orsatti, Mario. 2013. "Transcendental Meditation: Rx for Good Health." TM Blog. May 7, 2013. http://www.tm.org/blog/maharishi/transcendental-meditation-rx-for-good-health/.

32. Chawkin, Ken. 2011. "New study: TM Reduces Health Care Costs by 28%." TM Blog. October 10, 2011. http://www.tm.org/blog/research/healthcare/.

A Heavenly Haven for Health and Enlightenment

Enlightenment is for Everyone Blog. (2014, January 25). http://enlightenmentforeveryone.com/2014/01/25/ayurveda-health-enlightenment/

33. The Raj Ayurveda Health Spa: http://theraj.com

34. University of Maryland Medical Center. n.d. "Ayurveda." http://www.umm.edu/health/medical/altmed/treatment/ayurveda.

35. Maharishi Vastu® Architecture: Natural Law Based Design and Construction. Fortune-Creating® homes and buildings worldwide: http://www.maharishivastu.org

Section 4—Enlightenment

The Journey of Enlightenment—
You Don't Need to Go Anywhere

Huffington Post Blog. (2015, August 5). http://www.huffingtonpost.com/ann
-purcell/the-journey-ofenlightenm_1_b_7935088.html

1. Cheryl Strayed: http://www.cherylstrayed.com/wild_108676.htm
2. Transcendental Meditation: http://tm-women.org
3. Maharishi: http://enlightenmentforeveryone.com/maharishi-mahesh-yogi/

Enlightenment: The Missing Element

Yoga Dork Blog. (2015, June 26). http://yogadork.com/2015/06/26/enlighten
ment-the-missing-element/

4. Maharishi Mahesh Yogi. 1983. "Nourishing National Law by Enlivening
   Natural Law in National Consciousness." Filmed October 24, 1983 in
   Dublin, Ireland. Video. *Advanced Lectures on Maharishi's Transcendental
   Meditation Program, Volume 1.*
5. David Lynch Foundation. n.d. "The Quiet Time program: improving
   academic performance and reducing stress and violence."
   https://www.davidlynchfoundation.org/schools.html.
6. DeShannon, Jackie. 1965. "What The World Needs Now Is Love." Audio,
   3:10. Released April 15, 1965 by Imperial Records. Accessed online as
   Youtube video, posted September 2, 2012. https://www.youtube
   .com/watch?v=YUaxVQPohlU.

The Journey of Enlightenment

Huffington Post Blog. (2015, May 19). http://www.huffingtonpost.com/ann
-purcell/the-journey-of-enlightenm_b_7287024.html

7. Hsu, Christine. 2012. "Chilling Brain Scans Show the Impact of a
   Mother's Love on a Child's Brain Size." Medical Daily. October 29, 2012.
   http://www.medicaldaily.com/chilling-brain-scans-show-impact-mothers
   -love-childs-brain-size-243328.

   See also: Luby, Joan L., Deanna M. Barch, Andy Belden, Michael S.
   Gaffrey, Rebecca Tillman, Casey Babb, Tomoyuki Nishino, et al. 2012.
   "Maternal support in early childhood predicts larger hippocampal
   volumes at school age." *Proceedings of the National Academy of Sciences of
   the United States of America* 109, no. 8 (February): 2854-2859. doi: 10.1073/
   pnas.1118003109. https://www.ncbi.nlm.nih.gov/pmc/articles/PMC3286943.

8. Fowler, Joanna S., Nora D. Voldow, Cheryl A. Kassed, and Linda Chang. 2007. "Imaging the Addicted Human Brain." *Science and Practice Perspectives* 3, no. 2 (April): 4-16. doi: 10.1151/spp07324. https://www.ncbi.nlm.nih.gov/pmc/articles/PMC2851068/.

9. Transcendental Meditation for Women. n.d. "Scientific Research on the Transcendental Meditation program." http://www.tm-women.org/research-mental-potential.html.

10. Ball, Jeanne. 2010. "Keeping Your Prefrontal Cortex Online: Neuroplasticity, Stress and Meditation." Huffington Post Blog. August 11, 2010. http://www.huffingtonpost.com/jeanne-ball/keeping-your-prefrontal-c_b_679290.html.

11. Alexander, Charles N., Gerald C. Swanson, Maxwell V. Rainforth, Thomas W. Carlisle, Christopher C. Todd, and Robert M. Oates, Jr. 1993. "Effects of the Transcendental Meditation Program on Stress Reduction, Health, and Employee Development: A Prospective Study in Two Occupational Settings." *Anxiety, Stress, & Coping: An International Journal* 6, no. 3 (July): 245-262. doi: 10.1080/10615809308248383. http://www.tandfonline.com/doi/abs/10.1080/10615809308248383.

12. Research on Transcendental Meditation in schools:

    David Lynch Foundation: https://www.davidlynchfoundation.org/research.html

    Center for Wellness and Achievement in Education: http://cwae.org/research_intro.php

Are You Living Only Three of the Seven States of Consciousness?

Huffington Post Blog. (2015, October 2). http://www.huffingtonpost.com/ann-purcell/post_10262_b_8234634.html

13. Permanent Peace. n.d. "Transcendental Consciousness Objectively Verified." http://www.permanentpeace.org/technology/verified.html.

14. Wallace, Robert K. 1970. "Physiological Effects of Transcendental Meditation." *Science* 167, no. 3926 (March): 1751-1754. doi: 10.1126/science.167.3926.1751. https://www.ncbi.nlm.nih.gov/pubmed/5416544.

15. Chalmers, Roger. n.d. "Summary of Scientific Research on Maharishi's Transcendental Meditation and Transcendental Meditation-Sidhi Program." Truth About TM. Accessed July 2017. http://www.truthabouttm.org/truth/tmresearch/tmresearchsummary/index.cfm.

16. Truth about TM. n.d. "Cosmic Consciousness and Lucid Dreaming." http://
    www.truthabouttm.org/truth/TMResearch/NewStudies/Cosmic
    Consiousness/index.cfm.

    Mason, Lynn and David Orme-Johnson. 2010. "Transcendental
    Consciousness Wakes Up In Dreaming And Deep Sleep." *International
    Journal of Dream Research* 3, no. 1 (April): 28-32. http://dx.doi.org/10.11588/
    ijodr.2010.1.595. https://journals.ub.uni-heidelberg.de/index.php/IJoDR/
    article/view/595.

17. Maharishi Mahesh Yogi, *Science of Being and Art of Living* (Age of
    Enlightenment Publications, c1963; reprint, New York: Meridian, 1995), 80.

18. Pearson, Craig. 2010. "Ralph Waldo Emerson–Within Man Is The Soul
    Of The Whole; The Wise Silence; The Universal Beauty." TM Blog.
    September 27, 2010. http://www.tm.org/blog/enlightenment/ralph-waldo
    -emerson/.

19. Emerson, Ralph Waldo. 1841. "IX The Over-Soul." Accessed October 2015.
    http://www.rwe.org/complete/completeworks/ii-essays-i/iv-the-over
    -soul.html, para 3.

20. Maharishi on Youtube: https://www.youtube.com/user/maharishichannel

Enlightenment: More than Just a State of Mind

Enlightenment is for Everyone Blog. (2012, December 7). http://enlightenment
    foreveryone.com/2012/12/07/enlightenment-not-state-of-mind/

21. Wallace, Robert K. and Herbert Benson. 1972. "The Physiology of
    Meditation." *Scientific American* 226, no. 2 (February): 84-90. doi:10.1038/
    scientificamerican0272-84.

    Jevning, R., A.F. Wilson, J.P. O'Halloran, and R.N. Walsh 1983.
    "Forearm blood flow and metabolism during stylized and unstylized
    states of decreased activation." *American Journal of Physiology* 245, no. 1
    (July): R110-R116. https://www.ncbi.nlm.nih.gov/pubmed/6869572.

22. Dillbeck, Michael and Edward Bronson. 1981. "Short-term longitudinal
    effects of the Transcendental Meditation technique on EEG power
    and coherence." *International Journal of Neuroscience* 14, no. 3/4: 147-151.
    http://dx.doi.org/10.3109/00207458108985827. https://www.ncbi
    .nlm.nih.gov/pubmed/7030999.

23. Travis, Fred, Joe Tecce, Alarik Arenander, and R. Keith Wallace. 2002.
    "Patterns of EEG coherence, power and contingent negative variation
    characterize the integration of transcendental and waking states."
    Biological Psychology 61, no. 3 (November): 293-319. https://doi.org/

10.1016/S0301-0511(02)00048-0. https://www.ncbi.nlm.nih.gov/pubmed/12406612.

Travis, Fred and R. Keith Wallace. 1999. "Autonomic and EEG patterns during eyes-closed rest and Transcendental Meditation (TM) practice: a basis for a neural model of TM practice." *Consciousness and Cognition* 8, no. 3 (September): 302-318. https://doi.org/10.1006/ccog.1999.0403. https://www.ncbi.nlm.nih.gov/pubmed/10487785.

Travis, Fred and Alarik Arenander. 2006. "Cross-sectional and longitudinal study of effects of Transcendental Meditation practice on inter-hemispheric frontal asymmetry and frontal coherence." *International Journal of Neuroscience* 116, no. 12 (December): 1519-1538. doi: 10.1080/00207450600575482. https://www.ncbi.nlm.nih.gov/pubmed/17145686.

24. Travis, Fred and Jonathan Shear. 2010. "Focused attention, open monitoring and automatic self-transcending: Categories to organize meditations from Vedic, Buddhist and Chinese traditions." *Consciousness and Cognition* 19, no. 4 (December): 1110-1118. https://doi.org/10.1016/j.concog .2010.01.007. https://www.ncbi.nlm.nih.gov/pubmed/20167507.

25. Ask the Doctors. n.d. "Peer-Reviewed Scientific Journals publish the benefits of the Transcendental Meditation Technique." http://www .doctorsontm.org/tm-research/journals.

Section 5—Bliss and Silence

Bliss—Our Essential Nature

Enlightenment is for Everyone Blog. (2013, December 13). http://enlightenment foreveryone.com/2013/12/13/bliss-our-essential-nature/

1. Maharishi Mahesh Yogi, *Maharishi's Absolute Theory of Government* (India: Age of Enlightenment Publications, 1995), 39. Taittirīya Upanishad (3.6.1)

Follow Your Bliss

Huffington Post Blog. (2014, September 8). http://www.huffingtonpost.com/ann -purcell/folow-your-bliss_b_5053796.html

2. The Joseph Campbell Foundation. n.d. "About Joseph Campbell." https://www.jcf.org/about-joseph-campbell/ and https://www.jcf.org/about-joseph-campbell/follow-your-bliss/.

3. Michael Toms, *An Open Life: Joseph Campbell in Conversation with Michael Toms* (New York: Harper & Row, 1989), 24.

4. Transcendental Meditation for Women Professionals, "Scientific Research."

Bliss Is Not an Attitude

Daily Cup of Yoga. (2015, May 6). http://dailycupofyoga.com/2015/05/26/bliss-is-not-an-attitude/

The Silence Revolution

Huffington Post Blog. (2016, April 5). http://www.huffingtonpost.com/ann-purcell/the-silence-revolution_b_9612766.html

5. Cain, Susan. 2015. "How the Quiet Revolution Got Started." Huffington Post Blog. July 6, 2015. http://www.huffingtonpost.com/2015/07/06/how-the-quiet-revolution-got-started_n_7734868.html.

6. Huffington, Arianna. 2015. "Introducing HuffPost Quiet Revolution." *Huffington Post*, July 6, 2015. http://www.huffingtonpost.com/arianna-huffington/introducing-huffpost-quie_b_7732762.htm.

7. Permanent Peace, "Transcendental Consciousness Objectively Verified."

8. Travis and Shear, "Focused attention, open monitoring and automatic self-transcending: Categories to organize meditations from Vedic, Buddhist and Chinese traditions."

9. Travis, Frederick, Dave Haaga, John Hagelin, Melissa Tanner, Alarik Arenander, Sanford Nidich, Carolyn Gaylord-King, et al. 2010. "A Self-Referential Default Brain State: Patterns of Coherence, Power, and eLORETA Sources during Eyes-Closed Rest and Transcendental Meditation Practice." *Cognitive Processing* 11, no. 1 (February): 21-30. https://doi.org/10.1007/s10339-009-0343-2. https://www.ncbi.nlm.nih.gov/pubmed/19862565.

10. Travis and Arenander, "Cross-sectional and longitudinal study of effects of Transcendental Meditation practice on inter-hemispheric frontal asymmetry and frontal coherence."

11. David Lynch Foundation, "The Quiet Time program: improving academic performance and reducing stress and violence."

12. Global Union of Scientists for Peace. n.d. "The Brain-Based Approach to Peace." https://www.gusp.org/defusing-world-crises/brain-based-approach/.

The Power of Silence

Enlightenment is for Everyone Blog. (2014, February 28).
    http://enlightenmentforeveryone.com/2014/02/28/the-power-of-silence/

13. Travis, "The Transcendental Meditation technique and creativity: A
    longitudinal study of Cornell University undergraduates."

Twenty-Four Hours of Happiness

Huffington Post Blog. (2015, March 20). http://www.huffingtonpost.com/ann
    -purcell/24-hours-of-happiness_b_6798010.html

14. Williams, Pharrell. 2014. "Happiness Matters." *New York Times*,
    December 4, 2014. https://www.nytimes.com/2014/12/04/opinion/
    pharrell
    -williams-on-the-happy-phenomenon.html.
15. Centre for Bhutan studies & GNH. 2015. "Summary of 2015 Gross
    National Happiness Index." November 2015. http://www.grossnational
    happiness.com/SurveyFindings/Summaryof2015GNHIndex.pdf.

Happiness Runs in a Circular Motion

The Hidden Why Blog. (2016, September 3). http://www.thehiddenwhy.com/
    happiness-runs-circular-motion/

Section 6—Spiritual Reflections

Self-Empowerment

Enlightenment is for Everyone Blog. (2013, June 15). http://enlightenment
    foreveryone.com/2013/06/15/self-empowerment/

1. Mainquist, Linda. 2010. "New Research on the Meditating Brain." TM
    Blog. April 8, 2010. http://www.tm.org/blog/research/your-brain-and
    -transcendental-meditation-new-research/.
2. TM Women. "TM is a Successful Solution to PTSD with Veteran Supriya
    Vidic." Audio, 17:24. Accessed July 18, 2017. http://www.tm-women.org/first
    -responders/.
3. David Lynch Foundation. n.d. "David Lynch Foundation Women's Health
    Initiative." https://www.davidlynchfoundation.org/women.html.

Unconditioning: Beyond Labels

Huffington Post Blog. (2016, May 19). http://www.huffingtonpost.com/ann
-purcell/unconditioning-beyond-lab_1_b_10049384.html

4. Senghor, Shaka. 2016. "Shaka Senghor's Life Changing Epiphany."
   Interview by Oprah Winfrey. *Super Soul Sunday*, OWN, aired March 13,
   2016. http://www.oprah.com/own-super-soul-sunday/Shaka-Senghors-Life
   -Changing-Epiphany.

5. Prince Ea. 2016. "Prince Ea's Powerful Message About Labels." *Super Soul
   Sunday*, OWN, aired March 13, 2016. http://www.oprah.com/own-super
   -soul-sunday/A-Powerful-Message-About-Labels-by-Prince-Ea.

What I Know to Be True

Enlightenment is for Everyone Blog. (2017, October 24). http://enlightenment
foreveryone.com/2017/10/24/what-i-know-to-be-true/

The Deeper Meaning of Aloha

Enlightenment is for Everyone Blog. (2016, January 30). http://enlighten
mentforeveryone.com/2016/01/30/deeper-meaning-aloha/

6. University of Hawaii Community Colleges. n.d. "Aloha." http://www
   .uhcc.hawaii.edu/aloha/alohaSpirit.php.

7. Rule, Curby. n.d. "The Deeper Meaning of Aloha." Aloha International.
   http://www.huna.org/html/deeper.html.

Listen to Your Inner Voice

Selfgrowth.com. (2017, August 3). http://www.selfgrowth.com/articles/listen-to
-your-inner-voice

8. Winfrey, Oprah. 2011. "What Oprah Knows for Sure About Trusting Her
   Intuition." O, *The Oprah Magazine*, August 2011. http://www.oprah.com/
   spirit/oprah-on-trusting-her-intuition-oprahs-advice-on-trusting-your-gut.

9. David Lynch, *Catching the Big Fish*.

10. Oprah Winfrey, "What Oprah Knows for Sure About Trusting Her
    Intuition."

My Imagined Commencement Speech

Huffington Post Blog. (2015, June 23). http://www.huffingtonpost.com/ann
-purcell/my-imagined-commencement-_b_7638044.html

11. Winfrey, Oprah. 2013. "Oprah Winfrey Harvard Commencement
    speech." Filmed May 30, 2013 at Tercentenary Theatre, Harvard

University, Cambridge, MA. Youtube video, 28:58. Posted May 30, 2013. https://www.youtube.com/watch?v=GMWFieBGR7c.

12. Carrey, Jim. 2014. "Full Speech: Jim Carrey's Commencement Address at the 2014 MUM Graduation." Filmed May 24, 2014 at Maharishi University of Management, Fairfield, IA. Youtube video, 26:08. Posted May 30, 2014. https://www.youtube.com/watch?v=V80-gPkpH6M.

13. Hagelin, John. "John Hagelin: Is Consciousness the Unified Field?" Filmed at the Science and Non-Duality conference. Youtube video, 49:29. Posted July 19, 2014. https://www.scienceandnonduality.com/ videos/john-hagelin-is-consciousness-the-unified-field/.

Do You Believe in God?

Enlightenment is for Everyone Blog. (2017, July 28). http://enlightenment foreveryone.com/2017/07/28/do-you-believe-in-god/

14. OWN Network. 2012. "How Do Top Spiritual Thinkers Define God?" *Super Soul Sunday* (Season 4, Episode 306), OWN, aired December 16, 2012. http://www.oprah.com/own-super-soul-sunday/how-do-top-spiritual -thinkers-define-god-video.

Heaven—Now or Later?

Huffington Post Blog. (2015, December 16). http://www.huffingtonpost.com/ ann-purcell/heavennow-or-later_b_8806496.html

15. Maharishi Mahesh Yogi, *His Holiness Maharishi Mahesh Yogi, Thirty Years Around the World—Dawn of the Age of Enlightenment, Volume One 1957-1964* (Netherlands: MVU Press, 1986), 124.

16. Judith Wolfe and Brendan Wofe, *C.S. Lewis and the Church: Essays in Honor of Walter Hooper* (London: T&T Clark International, 2011), 105.

17. Transcendental Meditation. n.d. "What's the evidence?" http://www .tm.org/research-on-meditation.

18. Ann Purcell, *The Transcendental Meditation Technique and the Journey of Enlightenment* (Lake Worth, Florida: Green Dragon Books, 2015), 44.

From Darkness to Light

Enlightenment is for Everyone Blog. (2017, January 10). http://enlightenment foreveryone.com/2017/01/10/consciousness-darkness-light/

Ocean of Consciousness

Enlightenment is for Everyone Blog. (2017, September 26). http://enlight enmentforeveryone.com/2017/09/26/ocean-of-consciousness/

Section 7—Meditation

Meditation Versus Transcending

Enlightenment is for Everyone Blog. (2015, May 5). http://enlightenment
foreveryone.com/2015/05/11/meditation-vs-transcending/

1. Permanent Peace, "Transcendental Consciousness Objectively Verified."
2. Transcendental Meditation Asheville. n.d. "Brainwave Coherence During
   the Transcendental Meditation technique." http://meditation
   asheville.blogspot.com/2009/12/brainwave-coherence-during.html.

Are All Meditations the Same?

David Lynch Foundation Blog. (2015, August 25). http://www.davidlynchfoun
dation.org/blog/transcendental-meditation-different-forms-meditation/

3. Maharishi University of Management. "MUM's 'The Word': meditation."
   Youtube video, 7:00. Posted October 18, 2013. https://www
   .youtube.com/watch?v=yqekos9l59w.
4. LONI (Laboratory of Neuro Imaging). n.d. "Education: Brain Trivia."
   Accessed August 2015. http://www.loni.usc.edu/about_loni/
   education/brain_trivia.php.

Tim Ferriss, Dr. Tara Brach, and Some Misconceptions about Transcendental Meditation

Enlightenment is for Everyone Blog. (2016, February 18). http://enlighten
mentforeveryone.com/2016/02/18/tim-ferriss-brach-meditation/

5. Ferriss, Tim. 2015."Tara Brach Interview (Full Episode) | The Tim Ferriss
   Show (Podcast)." From *The Tim Ferriss Show,* July 31, 2015. Youtube video,
   2:08:41. Posted October 29, 2015. https://www.you
   tube.com/watch?v=pXNEM4wjSmE.
6. Ferriss, Tim. 2015. "Tara Brach on Meditation and Overcoming FOMO
   (Fear Of Missing Out)." *The Tim Ferriss Show,* July 31, 2015. Audio 2:08:05.
   https://tim.blog/2015/07/31/tara-brach/.
7. Maharishi University of Management. n.d. "Transcendental
   Consciousness." https://www.mum.edu/academics/research-institutes/
   center-for-brain-consciousness-and-cognition/transcendental
   -consciousness/.
8. Maharishi University of Management. n.d. "Cosmic Consciousness."
   https://www.mum.edu/academics/research-institutes/center-for-brain
   -consciousness-and-cognition/cosmic-consciousness/.

9. Purcell, *The Journey of Enlightenment*, 27.

10. Maharishi Mahesh Yogi, *Bhagavad Gita: A New Translation and Commentary* (Strand, London: Arkana, 1990), 331-332.

Can Listening to Music Help Me Transcend?

Enlightenment is for Everyone Blog. (2015, October 7). http://enlightenment foreveryone.com/2015/10/07/can-listening-to-music-help-me-transcend/

11. Thomas Carlyle. "The Hero as Poet." Lecture III, May 12, 1840. 83–84. Accessed online: http://www.online-literature.com/thomas-carlyle/heroes -and-hero-worship/3/.

How to Talk about Meditation to a Child

Enlightenment is for Everyone Blog. (2014, January 24). http://enlighten mentforeveryone.com/2014/01/24/maharishi-meditation-for-children/

12. Maharishi Mahesh Yogi. "Maharishi explains to children what Transcendental Meditation is." Youtube video, 4:53. Posted December 5, 2009. https://www.youtube.com/watch?v=2j7DKQU2dIo.

13. TM Women. n.d. "Children's Meditation." http://www.tm-women .org/childrens-meditation/.

Section 8—Yoga

In the Vicinity of Coherence (Yoga), Hostile Tendencies Are Eliminated

Enlightenment is for Everyone Blog. (2013, January 11). http://enlightenment foreveryone.com/2013/01/11/coherence-yoga-hostile-tendencies-eliminated/

1. Maharishi, *Maharishi's Absolute Theory of Government*, 516. Yoga Sutra (2.35)

2. "Sandy Hook Elementary School Shooting: Newtown, Connecticut Administrators, Students Among Victims, Reports Say." *Huffington Post*, December 14, 2012. http://www.huffingtonpost.com/2012/12/14/sandy -hook-elementary-school-shooting_n_2300831.html.

3. Maharishi, *Maharishi's Absolute Theory of Government*, 122.

4. Transcendental Meditation, "What's the evidence?"

International Yoga Day

Enlightenment is for Everyone Blog. (2015, June 19). http://enlightenment foreveryone.com/2015/06/19/intl-yoga-day/

5. Egenes, Thomas. 2010. "The Yoga Sutra and Deep Meditation." TM Blog. August 29, 2010. http://www.tm.org/blog/meditation/the-yoga-sutra-and -deep-meditation/.

6. Transcendental Meditation, "What's the evidence?"

7. International Day of Yoga: http://idayofyoga.org

8. Global Union of Scientists for Peace. n.d. "Scientific Research." https:// www.gusp.org/defusing-world-crises/scientific-research/.

9. Maharishi Mahesh Yogi, Global Press Conference. Filmed November 20, 2002, at Maharishi European Research University, Netherlands.

Want More than Downward Dog?

Enlightenment is for Everyone Blog. (2014, October 31). http://enlighten mentforeveryone.com/2014/10/31/yoga-enlightenment/

10. Smithsonian Institution, Freer/Sackler Gallery. *Yoga: The Art of Transformation.* Art Exhibit, October 2013 https://www.asia.si.edu/explore/yoga/.

11. Peter, J.C. 2013. "Yoga For Anger: 3 Moves To Help You Calm Down." Huffington Post Healthy Living. July 3, 2013. Originally published in *Spirituality and Health Magazine.* http://www.huffingtonpost.com/2013/07/ 03/yoga-for-anger_n_3536127.html.

12. Rodale, Maria. 2013. "Yoga for Improving Your Posture." Huffington Post Blog. July 23, 2013. http://www.huffingtonpost.com/maria-rodale/yoga-for -improving-your-p_b_3637374.html.

13. Gregoire, Carolyn. 2013. "12 Yoga Poses To Undo The Damage Of Your Desk Job." Huffington Post Healthy Living. June 18, 2013. http://www .huffingtonpost.com/2013/08/07/yoga-desk-job_n_3707818.html.

14. Rodale, Maria. 2013. "Yoga for Promoting Patience." Huffington Post Blog. June 18, 2013. http://www.huffingtonpost.com/maria-rodale/yoga-for -promoting-patien_b_3458603.html.

15. Norlyk Smith, Eva. 2013. "Yoga for Back Pain: Enhancing Body Awareness to Facilitate Healing." Huffington Post Blog. April 2, 2013. http://www.huffingtonpost.com/eva-norlyk-smith-phd/yoga-back-pain_b _2985805.html.

16. Bullock, B Grace. n.d. "More than a Short-Lived Fizz? Fizzy Yoga Targets Common Boomer Issues." YogaUOnline, 2013. https://www.yogau online.com/yogau-wellness-blog/more-short-lived-fizz-fizzy-yoga -targets-common-boomer-issues.

17. Dowdle, Hillarie. 2013. "How to Outsmart Your Insomnia: Can't sleep? Yoga practice and philosophy can help you let go and find rest." *Yoga Journal*, September 6, 2013. https://www.yogajournal.com/poses/sweet-surrender-3.

18. Berger, Jeremy. 2013. "10 Yoga Poses For Runners." Huffington Post Healthy Living. June 26, 2013. http://www.huffingtonpost.com/2014/06/26/yoga-for-runners_n_5507342.html. Originally published in *Men's Journal*.

19. "5 Pain-Relieving Yoga Poses." *Prevention*, November 16, 2011. http://www.prevention.com/fitness/yoga/yoga-poses-relieve-aches-and-pains.

20. "Broga? Yoga For Men Gets Its Own Name." Huffington Post Healthy Living. March 29, 2012. http://www.huffingtonpost.com/2012/03/28/broga-yoga-for-men_n_1385605.html.

21. Laughter Yoga University: https://laughteryoga.org

22. "Yoga For Older Adults: 5 Health Benefits Of The Practice For Post50s." *Huffington Post*. June 20, 2013. http://www.huffingtonpost.com/2013/05/20/yoga-older-adults_n_3268482.html.

23. Pearson, Catherine. 2013. "Toddler Yoga: Down Dog For Tots Is Here To Stay." Huffington Post. July 31, 2013. http://www.huffingtonpost.com/2013/07/31/toddler-yoga_n_2868905.html.

24. Maharishi, *Bhagavad Gita*, 331-332.

25. Egenes, "The Yoga Sutra and Deep Meditation."

26. MaharishiAustralia. "Maharishi Interview from 1965: Yoga & Transcendental Meditation." Youtube video, 4:45. Posted October 31, 2014. https://www.youtube.com/watch?v=aPXGgrlt9VM.

Yoga and Enlightenment

Enlightenment is for Everyone Blog. (2015, September 29). http://enlightenmentforeveryone.com/2015/09/29/yoga-enlightenment-2/

27. Woodyard, Catherine. 2011. "Exploring the therapeutic effects of yoga and its ability to increase quality of life." *International Journal of Yoga* 4, no. 2 (Jul-Dec): 49–54. http://doi.org/10.4103/0973-6131.85485. https://www.ncbi.nlm.nih.gov/pmc/articles/PMC3193654/.

Section 9—Women

Birds of a Feather Flock Together

Transcendental Meditation for Women. (2013, July 1). http://www.tm
-women.org/birds-of-a-feather-flock-together/

A United State of Women—Another Perspective

Huffington Post Blog. (2016, July 6). http://www.huffingtonpost.com/ann
-purcell/the-united-state-of-women_1_b_10723054.html

1. The United State of Women. "The United State of Women." Youtube
   video, 2:04. Posted June 6, 2016. https://www.youtube.com/watch?v
   =tFydoHotpes.

2. Rudolfsdottir, Annadis. 2005. "The Day the Women Went on Strike." *The
   Guardian*, October 18, 2005. https://www.theguardian.com/world/
   2005/oct/18/gender.uk.

3. Permanent Peace, "Transcendental Consciousness Objectively Verified."

4. International Center for Invincible Defense. n.d. "Scientific Foundation:
   The Unified Field." http://www.invincibledefense.org/approach.html.

5. Travis and Shear, "Focused attention, open monitoring and automatic self-
   transcending: Categories to organize meditations from Vedic, Buddhist and
   Chinese traditions."

6. Maharishi University of Management. n.d. "Summary of 13 published
   studies." https://www.mum.edu/about-mum/consciousness-based
   -education/tm-research/maharishi-effect/Summary-of-13-Published
   -Studies.

The Power of Women Gathering:
The Goddess is in Connections

Huffington Post Blog. (2017, January 5). http://www.huffingtonpost.com/ann
-purcell/the-power-of-women-gather_b_14367404.html

7. Taylor, Shelley E., Laura Cousino Klein, Brian P. Lewis, Tara L. Gruenewald,
   Regan A. R. Gurung, and John A. Updegraff. 2000. "Biobehavioral
   Responses to Stress in Females: Tend-and-Befriend, Not Fight-or-Flight."
   Psychological Review 107, no. 3: 411–429. University of California, Los
   Angeles. https://scholar.harvard.edu/marianabockarova/files/tend-and
   -befriend.pdf.

Buddhist School for Girls in Thailand

Huffington Post Blog. (2013, July 31). http://www.huffingtonpost.com/ann
-purcell/thailand-buddhist-education_b_3683746.html

8. Dhammajarinee Witthaya School: http://www.thaischool.org
9. David Lynch Foundation. "TM at Dhammajarinee School in Northern
Thailand." Youtube video, 6:03. Posted May 27, 2015. https://www
.youtube.com/watch?v=eCd7CfME2J8.

Section 10—Environment

Inner Sustainability: A New Concept for Earth Day

Huffington Post Blog. (2014, April 18). http://www.huffingtonpost.com/ann
-purcell/celebrating-earth-day-mot_b_5153302.html

1. City of Philadelphia. n.d. "Office of Sustainability." Accessed April 2014.
https://beta.phila.gov/departments/office-of-sustainability/.
2. "Top 10 Green U.S. Cities." Mother Nature Network. October 16, 2009.
https://www.mnn.com/health/allergies/photos/top-10-green-us-cities/what
-makes-a-city-green.
3. Guest Contributor. 2013. "Top 10 Greenest Cities in the World." The Green
Optimistic. June 4, 2013. https://www.greenoptimistic.com/top-10-greenest
-cities-20130604/#.WWrLFTOZP64.
4. Hagelin, John. 2011. "Is Consciousness the Unified Field? with Dr. John
Hagelin." Interview by Peter Tongue. *Awakening to Conscious Co-Creation*,
VoiceAmerica Internet Talk Radio, December 28, 2011. Audio, 55:24. https://
www.voiceamerica.com/episode/58427/is-consciousness-the-unified-field
-with-dr-john-hagelin.
5. Bergman, Jackie. "Meditation and sustainability: John Hagelin, Professor
in Quantum Physics." Youtube video, 8:35. Posted March 18, 2013. https://
www.youtube.com/watch?v=aV3pQMquGFY.
6. Maharishi, *Science of Being and Art of Living*, 164.
7. Purcell, Ann. "Mother Earth Music Video." Youtube video, 3:42. Posted
March 24, 2014. https://www.youtube.com/watch?v=m3eBPs_wUog.

Global Interconnectedness—Holistic Solutions

Enlightenment is for Everyone Blog. (2013, January 16). http://enlighten
mentforeveryone.com/2013/01/16/global-interconnectedness-holistic
-solutions/

8. Let's Move! America's Move to Raise A Healthier Generation of Kids: https://letsmove.obamawhitehouse.archives.gov

9. Mercola, Joseph. 2011. "The 9 Foods the U.S. Government is Paying You to Eat." Mercola. August 3, 2011. http://articles.mercola.com/sites/articles/archive/2011/08/03/the-9-foods-the-us-government-is-paying-you-to-eat.aspx.

10. Henson, Bob. 2012. "Phenomenon of the Year: Sandy's Stunning Surge: What made the threat so complex, and so hard to communicate?" The University Corporation for Atmospheric Research: Atmos News. December 31, 2012. https://www2.ucar.edu/atmosnews/perspective/8584/phenomenon-year-sandy-s-stunning-surge.

Prince Charles—a Visionary Leader

Enlightenment is for Everyone Blog. (2016, November 30). http://enlightenmentforeveryone.com/2016/11/30/prince-charles-visionary-leader/

11. Prince Charles, Prince of Wales: https://www.princeofwales.gov.uk

12. H.R.H. Prince of Wales, Tony Juniper, and Ian Skelly, *Harmony: A New Way of Looking at Our World* (Great Britain: HarperCollins, 2010).

13. The Harmony Movie. "HARMONY (Teaser)." Youtube video, 4:04. Posted April 26, 2010. https://www.youtube.com/watch?v=iWJtS2VpYm0.

Prince Charles, Part 1: The Age of Disconnection and Ideal Housing

Enlightenment is for Everyone Blog. (2016, November 30). http://enlightenmentforeveryone.com/2016/11/30/prince-charles-visionary-leader/

14. H.R.H. Prince of Wales, *Harmony*, 12.

15. Ibid., 19.

16. Ibid., 89.

17. Maharishi Vastu Architecture: Natural Law Based Design and Construction. n.d. "Principles of Maharishi Vastu Architecture." http://www.maharishivastu.org/principles-of-maharishi-vastu-architecture.

18. Institute of Vedic City Planning: Architecture and Urban Design in Harmony with Natural Law. (n.d). "Worldwide Projects." http://www.vediccityplanning.com/institute/worldwide-projects/.

19. Maharishi Vastu Architecture, "Principles of Maharishi Vastu Architecture."

Prince Charles, Part 2: The Age of Disconnection and Holistic Education

Enlightenment is for Everyone Blog. (2016, December 2). http://enlighten mentforeveryone.com/2016/12/02/prince-charles-holistic-education/

20. H.R.H. Prince of Wales, *Harmony*, 147.

21. Ibid., 149.

22. Ibid., 150.

23. The Prince's School of Traditional Arts: https://www.psta.org.uk

24. Consciousness-Based Education: https://consciousnessbasededucation .org/

25. Maharishi University of Management: https://www.mum.edu

26. Maharishi School: http://www.maharishischooliowa.org

27. Maharishi University of Management. n.d. "The Sustainable Living Center Building." https://www.mum.edu/academic-departments/sustainable -living/sl-building/.

    Micah Sallaberios. "The Sustainable Living Center." Youtube video, 2:37. Posted October 11, 2012. https://www.youtube.com/watch?v=dcbjB_JwU5c.

28. Maharishi Vastu® Architecture: Natural Law Based Design and Construction. https://www.maharishivastu.org/

Prince Charles, Part 3: The Age of Disconnection, Holistic Health and Environmental Awareness

Enlightenment is for Everyone Blog. (2016, December 6). http://enlighten mentforeveryone.com/2016/12/06/prince-charles-harmony-holistic-health -environment/

29. Gray, Louise. 2010. "The Prince of Wales begins project to protect area of rainforest the size of Wales." *The Telegraph*, September 2010. http://www .telegraph.co.uk/news/earth/prince-of-wales-start/7987910/The-Prince-of -Wales-begins-project-to-protect-area-of-rainforest-the-size-of-Wales.html.

30. National Resources Defense Council. n.d. "Global Warming 101." https:// www.nrdc.org/stories/global-warming-101.

31. Peace Trees. "The Book & Film: Harmony: A New Way of Looking at the World.—A sustainable revolution." Youtube video, 6:33. Posted November 10, 2010. https://www.youtube.com/watch?v=bXr7aUxvvbA.

32. Taparia, Hans, and Pamela Koch. 2015. "A Seismic Shift in How People Eat." *New York Times*, November 6, 2015. https://www.nytimes.com/2015/ 11/08/opinion/a-seismic-shift-in-how-people-eat.html.

33. Maharishi Mahesh Yogi, *Maharishi's Master Plan to Create Heaven on Earth* (The Netherlands: Maharishi Vedic University Press, 1991), 25.

34. H.R.H. Prince of Wales, *Harmony*, 306.

GMOs: Are We Crossing the Tipping Point?

Huffington Post Blog. (2015, June 11). http://www.huffingtonpost.com/ann -purcell/gmos_b_7547414.html

35. Chipotle Mexican Grill, Inc. n.d. "Chipotle—A Farewell to GMOs. Food With Integrity: G-M-Over it." https://www.chipotle.com/gmo.

36. Smith, Aaron. 2015. "Pizza Hut and Taco Bell to remove artificial ingredients." CNN. May 26, 2015. http://money.cnn.com/2015/05/26/news/ companies/taco-bell-pizza-hut-similac/.

37. Gram, Dave. 2015."Vermont Law on GMO Labels Stands." U.S. News. April 27, 2015. https://www.usnews.com/news/us/articles/2015/04/27/food -industry-tries-to-block-vermonts-gmo-labeling-law.

38. Cressey, Daniel. 2015. "Widely Used Herbicide Linked to Cancer." Scientific American, *Nature*, March 25, 2015. https://www. scientificamerican.com/article/widely-used-herbicide-linked-to-cancer/.

39. "Sri Lanka's New President Puts Immediate Ban on Glyphosate Herbicides." Sustainable Pulse. May 25, 2015. http://sustainablepulse.com/ 2015/05/25/sri-lankas-new-president-puts-immediate-ban-on-glypho sate-herbicides/7/#.WWuXAzOZNcA.

40. Louv, Jason. 2017. "The World vs. Monsanto: A Short History of the Battle Against the Most Evil Corporation on the Planet." Ultra Culture. April 21, 2017. https://ultraculture.org/blog/2017/04/21/monsanto/.

Section 11—Gifts of Nature

Mango Season Has Arrived

Enlightenment is for Everyone Blog. http://enlightenmentforeveryone.com/ 2016/07/13/mango-season/

1. Truly Tropical Mango Orchard: http://delraymango.blogspot.com

2. Morris, Michele. "Benefits of Eating What's in Season." Gaiam Blog. https://www.gaiam.com/blogs/discover/benefits-of-eating-what-s-in -season.

3. Ibid.

4. Ware, Megan. 2015. "Mangoes: Health Benefits, Nutritional Breakdown." Medical News Today. October 21, 2015. http://www.medicalnewstoday.com/articles/275921.php.

Papaya and Other Exotic Fruits

Enlightenment is for Everyone Blog. (2016, January 26). http://enlightenment foreveryone.com/2016/01/26/papaya-kauai-hawaii/

Gwyneth Paltrow and Chocolate Mousse

Huffington Post Blog. (2016, August 9). http://www.huffingtonpost.com/ann -purcell/gwyneth-paltrow-and-choco_b_11353954.html

5. Gwyneth Paltrow and Thea Baumann, *It's All Easy: Delicious Weekday Hacks for the Super-busy Home Cook* (Boston, MA: Life & Style, 2016).

6. Gwyneth Paltrow's lifestyle website: http://goop.com/

May—Florida at Its Best

Enlightenment is for Everyone Blog. (2016, May 19). http://enlightenment foreveryone.com/2016/05/19/may-florida-best/

FOR MORE INFORMATION

- Enlightenment is for Everyone
  www.enlightenmentforeveryone.com

- The Transcendental Meditation technique and how to learn:
  www.TM-women.org
  www.TM.org

- Programs for women and the ladies' wing of the Transcendental
  Meditation organization:
  www.tmwomenprofessionals.org
  www.globalwomensorganization.org
  www.globalhealthfoundationforwomen.org

- Maharishi University of Enlightenment, which offers degree programs for ladies:
  www.maharishiuniversityofenlightenment.com

- The Mother Divine Program:
  www.motherdivine.org

- Maharishi University of Management:
  www.mum.edu

- Maharishi School of the Age of Enlightenment:
  www.maharishischooliowa.org

- The David Lynch Foundation for Consciousness-Based Education
  and World Peace:
  www.davidlynchfoundation.org

- News of positive trends rising in the world:
  www.globalgoodnews.com

- The Global Peace Initiative:
  www.globalpeaceinitiative.org

SUGGESTED READING

- *Science of Being and Art of Living—Transcendental Meditation* by Maharishi Mahesh Yogi
- *Maharishi Mahesh Yogi on the Bhagavad-Gita: A New Translation and Commentary, Chapters 1–6* by Maharishi Mahesh Yogi
- *Love and God* by Maharishi Mahesh Yogi
- *The TM Book: How to Enjoy the Rest of Your Life* by Denise Denniston
- *Strength in Stillness* by Bob Roth
- *Transcendence: Healing and Transformation through Transcendental Meditation* by Dr. Norman Rosenthal
- *Super Mind: How to Boost Performance and Live a Richer and Happier Life Through Transcendental Meditation* by Dr. Norman Rosenthal
- *Catching the Big Fish: Meditation, Consciousness, and Creativity* by David Lynch
- *The Neurophysiology of Enlightenment* by Dr. Robert Keith Wallace
- *The Supreme Awakening: Experiences of Enlightenment Throughout Time—and How You Can Cultivate Them* by Craig Pearson

ABOUT THE AUTHOR

Ann Purcell is the award-winning author of *The Transcendental Meditation Technique and the Journey of Enlightenment*. Her second book, *Tender Flower of Heaven*, is a collection of 130 poems. She is a songwriter and has released 7 CDs, is a regular contributor to the Huffington Post, and has been featured in many podcast and radio interviews.

Ann has been a full-time teacher of Transcendental Meditation since 1973, teaching Transcendental Meditation and advanced courses in many countries around the world. In addition, she has worked on curricula and course development for universities and continuing education programs. She oversees the teaching of Transcendental Meditation in girls' schools and communities in several countries in Africa. She has a BSCI (Bachelor of the Science of Creative Intelligence) and an MSCI from Maharishi European Research University, Seelisberg, Switzerland. She received a PhD in Supreme Political Science from Maharishi University of World Peace, Vlodrop, Netherlands.

Connect with Ann Purcell

Ann would enjoy hearing from you with any questions or comments. You can contact her online at:

http://www.enlightenmentforeveryone.com/contact/

Read blog posts about enlightenment, health, world peace, and more at:

http://www.enlightenmentforeveryone.com/blog
http://www.huffingtonpost.com/ann-purcell/

Facebook: http://www.facebook.com/Enlightenmentforeveryone

Twitter: http://twitter.com/purcell_ann

Youtube: http://www.youtube.com/enlightenmentbook

Made in the USA
Columbia, SC
24 April 2018